Little, Brown and Company
Hachette Book Group
237 Park Avenue, New York, NY 10017
www.hachettebookgroup.com

First Edition: October 2010

Little, Brown and Company is a division of Hachette Book Group, Inc. The Little, Brown name and logo are trademarks of Hachette Book Group, Inc.

The Peanuts Collection is produced by becker&mayer!, Bellevue, WA.
www.beckermayer.com

Design: Todd Bates
Editorial: Amy Wideman
Image Research: Chris Campbell
Production Coordination: Leah Finger
License Acquisition: Josh Anderson

ISBN 978-0-316-08610-3
LCCN 2010924129

10 9 8 7 6 5 4 3 2 1

Printed in China

Contents

Foreword

Growing up, as far as I was concerned, my dad was not Snoopy's father; he was my father. I remember having Peanuts comic books around the house and products like the Hungerford dolls (see page 13), pillows, toys, and pennants. I used to love going into his office with my sister and our friends, opening the special drawers that held a few of these items and choosing a Peanuts sweatshirt to wear. I also have vivid memories of sitting on my dad's lap as he read his comic books to me. Every so often, he would laugh at one of his strips. I remember thinking, "Well, of course you think this is funny, you wrote it!" even though I thought they were funny too.

Back then I wasn't quite convinced he had a "real job." He didn't go off to work like other dads did; he worked in a studio right on our property. He never worked past 5 o'clock, nor on weekends. If any one of his children wanted to visit with him, we would think nothing of walking into the studio, right past the secretary, and straight to his office. To this day, I can picture him looking up as I walked in the room and immediately putting down his pen to talk to me. He never once asked me to wait just a minute while he finished a drawing or some lettering. Whenever my brothers interrupted him in the middle of the day and asked him to play baseball, he happily complied. As much as he loved the strip, he loved his children even more.

On October 2, 1950, he signed with United Feature Syndicate, with the belief and knowledge that his job was to help editors sell newspapers. On that day, it was only seven papers. Fifty years later, with the strip setting a world record at 2,600 newspapers, Dad still went to work motivated by that same belief: that his job was simply to help the editor sell his paper.

As a child, I didn't really understand how much talent he had, and how hard he'd worked to develop it. As an adult, I can see that he knew both his skills and his limitations; he admired and studied the talents of other artists. His pen lines were everything and he was proud of the work he turned in every week. He would often remind me that it was his job to draw something funny every day, meaning that it was not just the punch line or the story that was important, but also the humor of the drawings themselves.

Life gives birth to pure art and a true artist pays attention to the details around him—not just the details in *his* life, but in *all* life. My dad's gift for observation was proven by the fact that hundreds of millions of people throughout the world would wake up every morning and turn the newspaper page to *his* strip—nearly 18,000 strips in all—because they had grown to love the characters as real people.

My dad believed that he was born to draw his comic strip, and his fans refer to him as a genius. If he is a genius, then I believe it is because of his ability to create characters that were loved as though they were real, and to draw fifty years' worth of strips that had relevance in the lives of millions of people.

— Amy Schulz Johnson

A Note from the Author

Peanuts has played a role in my life for longer than I can even remember. My first exposure may have been my mother calling me "Charlie Brown." (Admittedly, she called all of her children "Charlie Brown," which saved her from having to remember which kid she was talking to.) Or perhaps it was catching *A Charlie Brown Thanksgiving* on TV, or finding that book of strips my brother had bought at a yard sale. Whatever the trigger was, it started an enduring relationship with characters whose joys and fears I understood and recognized in my own. I'm hardly alone in this; millions of people around the globe hold Peanuts in a special place. They may not have gone as over the top about it as I have (not everyone owns a thousand Peanuts-related books, runs a Peanuts-themed website, or appears in documentaries about Peanuts), but whether it's wearing a little silver Schroeder on their charm bracelet, getting a smile out of a Snoopy greeting card, or enjoying a family tradition of huddling around *A Charlie Brown Christmas* each year, Peanuts is something that has touched them.

Peanuts' influence can be seen in almost every modern comic strip, and in a vast number of cultural references, all around the world. The strip that Charles Schulz so lovingly crafted over the course of half a century is a thing of beauty in itself, but it has also provided rich soil from which so much else has bloomed. This book examines that richness, looks at the masterfully simple lines and dots of ink that make up

the characters on the page, the animation that brings them life, and the way they've moved beyond the page and screen to other parts of our world. It shows the basis for things so many have loved for so many decades.

Building this book involved going through the archives of Peanuts material, finding interesting items—many never before seen by the public—to share. I got to interview people who worked with Schulz, people he knew and loved, and many others whose lives have felt the impact of Peanuts. I found much that was joyful along the way, and I hope these words, pictures, and items bring you joy as well.

— Nat Gertler

FEATURED: Voicing his thoughts on the strip's title in a letter to United Feature Syndicate dated October 30, 1957, Schulz references notes like the one shown at center left.

Charles M. Schulz

To the people who read *Peanuts* in the daily paper, his name was simply "Schulz," written in a quick, clear hand along the edge of one of the panel borders. Those who read the books knew him by the more complete name "Charles M. Schulz." But to friends and family he was always "Sparky," taken from the nickname of the cartoon horse "Spark Plug" that had been introduced into the then-popular comic strip *Barney Google* in 1922, the year that Charles Monroe Schulz was born.

An only child, Schulz was bright yet shy. He was a big fan of the comics pages, poring over them with his father and learning to copy the characters on his own. (When later asked about whether he was surprised by his success, he'd confess, "It was something that I had planned for since I was six years old.") In school, other students would have him draw Popeye or other characters on their notebooks. He first landed in the funny pages himself when he was fourteen, when a drawing he did of family dog Spike was included in the *Ripley's Believe It or Not!* feature. He continued to train as an artist, with his father going into debt to pay for a correspondence class from Federal Schools (now known as Art Instruction Schools—the same folks who invite you to draw Tippy the Turtle).

Schulz started submitting cartoons for publication just after high school, but as with the plans of so many other young men of the day, war got in the way. He was drafted into the Army during World War II, serving most of his three-year stint leading a machine gun squad in Europe. After his discharge, he didn't have a job waiting, and at first he turned to small art jobs, almost accepting a job lettering tombstones. Luckily, his art career grew, going from lettering the dialog on others' art for the Catholic comic book *Topix* to providing original single-panel gag cartoons for them and for local newspapers. He returned to the Art Instruction Schools, this time as an employee, grading students' assignments.

In 1947 he hit the big time, landing his first cartoon in the *Saturday Evening Post*. In *The Book of Knowledge Annual 1966*, Schulz would warn that magazine cartoonists "can fall into the trap of imitating the host of cartoonists who draw the many anonymous characters with the same-type noses, half-closed eyes, and smug expressions that we see in practically every magazine"—but in the seventeen cartoons he did for the *Post*, it was clear that he had his own very distinct style, as well as his own themes.

In 1950, Schulz was a single man in his late twenties, no longer a child and not yet a parent—but with enough drawing talent and enough insight about humanity to launch *Peanuts*, a strip very much focused on children. He would marry Joyce Halverson in 1951 and go on to raise five kids with her. After their marriage dissolved in the early 1970s, he would wed again, this time to Jean Forsyth Clyde, for a marriage that would last the rest of his life. He would try other comic strip projects, including the short-lived feature *It's Only a Game* and a series of single-panel gags for Christian youth magazines. Yet for the almost fifty years that he spent creating them, Schulz's life would be primarily devoted to his little people—his Peanuts. With his lively line and wonderful ear for dialogue, he gave them life in a way that has moved millions.

OPPOSITE PAGE: (top left) A collection of humorous self-portraits; (bottom left) Schulz with boyhood pup, Spike, ca 1940. **THIS PAGE:** (top right) The artist at his drawing board, ca 1956; (bottom right) Schulz's lifelong nickname was borrowed from Barney Google's horse, seen in this panel from the day Schulz was born.

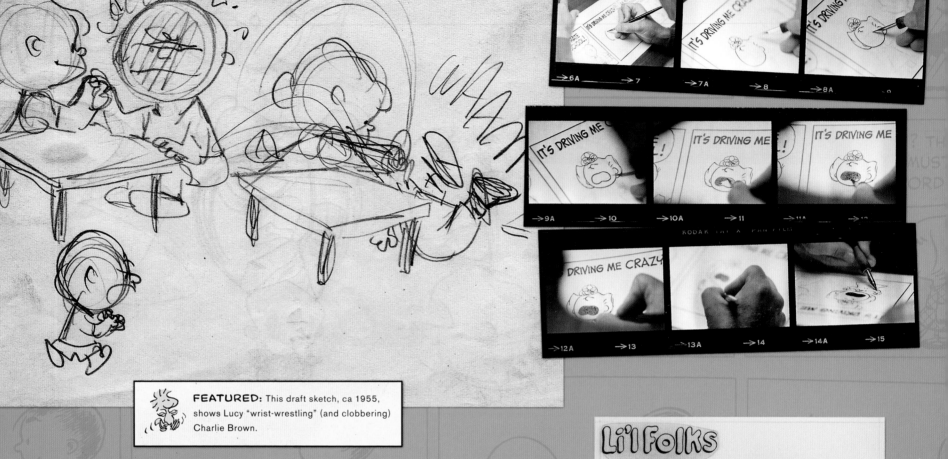

FEATURED: This draft sketch, ca 1955, shows Lucy "wrist-wrestling" (and clobbering) Charlie Brown.

Li'l Folks
BY SPARKY

"THE WHOLE TROUBLE WITH YOU IS THAT YOUR EYES ARE BIGGER THAN YOUR STOMACH!"

"THERE HE GOES...OUT OF MY LIFE FOREVER...I'LL PROBABLY MISS HIM A LOT AT FIRST, BUT BY THREE O'CLOCK I SHOULD BE OVER IT...."

Peanuts in Strips

For years prior to the debut of *Peanuts*, Schulz had been doing single-panel cartoons and *Li'l Folks*, his feature in Minnesota newspapers. In some ways, *Li'l Folks* was like *Peanuts*—the cartoons were about children, and no adults were ever seen—but in many ways it was quite different. There were no continuing characters in these single-panel gags, and although there were four appearances by a "Charlie Brown" (a name Schulz borrowed from a coworker), each time it was for a different character.

Schulz's goal was to sell *Li'l Folks* into a national market. United Feature Syndicate was interested in distributing Schulz's work, but they weren't interested in single-panel gags. They wanted strips, and with them, continuing characters. Due to potential legal conflicts, they also wanted a new title. By the time the work was renamed and distributed, li'l remained of *Li'l Folks*.

That format change, as it turned out, would be a tremendous boon not only to Schulz, but to comics as a whole. While single-gag panels were amusing, an ongoing strip allowed Schulz to create characters who would grow and evolve, becoming people readers would recognize and care about. It allowed him to tell stories, rather than just capture moments. And it fostered a work that proved inspirational to most of the great strips of the past half century.

When the syndicate first began pitching *Peanuts* to newspapers, they touted convenience more than anything else. (Because of its multipanel makeup, the strip could be stacked and resized in various ways to fill whatever hole an editor had in his pages.) Apparently that wasn't a blockbuster selling point; only seven papers picked up the strip for its launch. It was after the quality of content *inside* those rearrangeable panels became apparent that the strip caught on. *Peanuts* went on to run for fifty years—in sum, well over 17,000 daily installments, all created by Schulz. Along the way, it set multiple records for the number of newspapers carrying it.

When Schulz fell ill in late 1999, the run of new installments came to an end. And while some comics outlive their original creators, the *Peanuts* strip and Schulz could not be separated. Readers immediately made it clear to the newspapers that they wanted to see Charlie Brown, Snoopy, and the rest of the crew every day, even if the installment wasn't brand-new. Today, *Peanuts* continues to enjoy a prominent place in over 2,200 newspapers.

OPPOSITE PAGE: (top right) Schulz inking Sally during a 1969 photo shoot for *Charlie Brown and Charles Schulz*; (bottom row) a *Peanuts* from the strip's first month, and two *Li'l Folks* samples created as pitch materials for national syndication. **THIS PAGE:** (enclosure) "The Peanuts Album," a promotional booklet ca 1953 featuring Schulz and his early characters. Newspapers advertised that fans could write in to receive a copy. (bottom right) Another piece of *Li'l Folks* art.

1950s 1960s 1970s 1980s 1990s

Charlie Brown

It was Charlie Brown's world from the very beginning. Since the debut strip—when readers learned his name courtesy of the two children gossiping about him—through a fifty-year run in which new characters, new quirks, and even new neighborhoods were added, Charlie Brown, his family, his friends, and his turf have remained the comic's core.

When the series kicked off in October 1950, he wasn't yet the lovable loser that he would come to be. The original Charlie Brown was a bit of a joker, a bit more confident (in the later years it would've been odd to see him refer to his "happy, carefree school days" as he did early on). But as the rather generic characters of the early days (Shermy and Patty) were joined and eventually supplanted by more-defined personalities (Schroeder, Linus, Lucy, and others), Charlie Brown became the (relatively) sane center. He was notable not just for his tendency to fail at achieving his goals, but for his willingness to keep on trying: trying to win that ball game, to fly that kite, to trick-or-treat and get candy instead of rocks. Whether that's seen as an admirable stick-to-itiveness or an all but flat learning curve, his ability to let hope outweigh more pragmatic instincts is one that almost everybody can empathize with. In one way or another, we all keep trying to kick that football, no matter how many times it's pulled away from us.

The little boy with the big round head grew up the way Peanuts characters do—slowly, unevenly, and eventually hitting a maximum age. He was about four years old at the beginning of the strip, and the shortest of his small group. He soon gained his trademark zigzagged shirt—a novel contrast to his single curlycue of hair.

It was only in the cartoon sphere that Charlie Brown failed to get respect. In the real world, he was a star. His name probably should have been in the title of the strip; it wound up in the title of almost everything related to it. Most of the TV specials and movies bear his name, and for years the same was true of the books that reprinted the strips. (And if his name wasn't headlining, his dog's probably was.) Beginning in November of 1966, the big title space on the Sunday strips grew from simply *Peanuts* to *Peanuts featuring 'Good Ol' Charlie Brown'* (regardless of whether he actually appeared in that installment). In the grand scheme, Charlie Brown earned admiration from everyone—everyone but a certain little red-haired girl.

THIS PAGE: (top left) Schulz sketches Charlie Brown reading the *Mirror Daily News* with Snoopy, ca 1959; (top right) the little round-headed boy's evolution; (center) an unfinished strip ca late–1950s. OPPOSITE PAGE: (left) Schulz demonstrates for the camera in December 1956; (right) a kind word from Dr. Spock; (bottom right) peers introduce "good ol'" Charlie Brown.

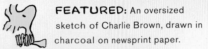

FEATURED: An oversized sketch of Charlie Brown, drawn in charcoal on newsprint paper.

BENJAMIN SPOCK, M. D.
2040 ABINGTON ROAD
CLEVELAND 6, OHIO

September 26, 1956

Mr. Schulz
Peanuts Comic Strip
United Features Syndicate
The Press
Rockwell Avenue & East 9th
Cleveland, Ohio

Dear Mr. Schulz:

You can tell Charlie Brown for me that I care for him
very much.

Sincerely,

Benjamin Spock

Benjamin Spock, M.D.

PEANUTS®

5331 49¢

Pictures to Color

FEATURED: Selected pages from *Peanuts Pictures to Color*, one of a series published in the 1960s.

featuring 16 page STORY BOOKLET illustrated in color

PEANUTS®

21 VIEW·MASTER stereo pictures

DISCO SNOOPY COLORFORMS SET

colorforms

Create your own Peanuts Disco with Colorforms Plastic that Sticks like Magic!!!

GAME B

MISS 3 68

Snoopy knocks down the flying musical notes so they won't wake Woodstock.

Nintendo Co.,Ltd.

SNOOPY

TABLETOP

Nintendo

Playtime

Peanuts may be about kids, but Schulz always considered his real audience to be adults. Still, the philosophical themes of the strip never stood in the way of kids' enjoyment, and where there are kids, there will be toys and games and other things to play with.

The toys began in 1958, when Hungerford Plastics manufactured pint-sized versions of Charlie Brown, Snoopy, Lucy, Linin, Sally, and Schroeder. In spite of this being the first stab at a 3-D depiction of the characters, they were remarkably well rendered. Board games followed soon after, and the march was on.

Since that time, the Peanuts characters have appeared on all manner of playthings—toy drums, sno-cone machines, video games, you name it. They've merged with major playtime brands to give us products like Snoopy Monopoly, A Charlie Brown Christmas Uno, It's the Great Pumpkin Charlie Brown Yahtzee, and even a boxed set with

Snoopy and Barbie both dressed as World War I Flying Aces. Some Peanuts toys have encouraged kids to create, building scenes using Colorforms characters or homemade moldable figures made of a substance called "Plasti-Goop." Stuffed Snoopies have ranged from pocket-sized pups to versions too big to fit into a typical doghouse, and Peanuts plushes have modeled all sorts of creative getups, from nightgowns to medical scrubs to camping gear.

A Peanuts toy can seem like a small thing, but small things have a way of staying with us. Consider young Mike: He was six in 1969 when his big brother, ten years his senior, gave him a Snoopy doll dressed as an astronaut. Man had just landed on the moon, so the spacesuit was especially appealing to a population tuned into extraterrestrial possibilities.

Mike didn't stay young forever, of course. He outgrew many things, but he never outgrew his love for Snoopy, nor his love for space flight. The years weren't always kind to the toy: he suffered a broken leg and, more significantly to an astronaut, his little life-support pack got lost, as did the bubble dome designed to protect him out in space. Snoopy would not seem to be fit to be an astronaut any longer. And yet . . .

Little Mike ended up becoming Michael J. Massimino, a highly trained and accomplished engineer, an assistant professor . . . and an astronaut. When the space shuttle Atlantis went up in May of 2009 on the final servicing mission for the Hubble space telescope, Mike was onboard, and he brought his little Snoopy doll along, floating in zero gravity with all the rest of the crew.

OPPOSITE PAGE: Over the years, Peanuts has graced everything from activity sets to View-Masters to handheld video games. **THIS PAGE:** (top left) The characters' first foray into 3-D in 1958, courtesy of Hungerford Plastics; (top right) Milton Bradley's 1972 Peanuts board game; (bottom left) two sought-after Peanuts lunch boxes, ca 1974 (left) and 1968.

Halloween

Peanuts certainly enjoys some endearing and enduring links to Christmas, but its links to Halloween are arguably more important. In subtle but lasting ways, the comic may have actually shaped the modern experience of the holiday.

Halloween was a big deal in the strip during its early years, with trick-or-treating plots and funny costumes and jack-o'-lantern gags frequently providing more strips than Christmas in a given year. And in 1959, Schulz devised the engine that would run the Halloween strips for a long time to come: Linus's letter to "The Great Pumpkin," which included a list of toys he hoped to receive for Halloween. The sequence ran for about a week, with Linus spinning the tale of The Great Pumpkin and wanting to go out and sing "pumpkin carols." As Halloween passed with no sign of presents, Linus came to realize that he was "a victim of false doctrine."

It was too good a concept to abandon, however, for both Linus and Schulz. The next year, The Great Pumpkin storyline ran more than two full weeks, and the concept of waiting out in a pumpkin patch (a "sincere" pumpkin patch) for The Great Pumpkin's arrival was introduced.

The Great Pumpkin was never actually seen and thus not part of the visual imagery for the holiday, but the image of a young boy waiting out in a pumpkin patch on a chilly October night became a powerfully affecting symbol. Whereas Halloween imagery is usually scary in nature—evil witches, bats, skeletons, leering jack-o'-lanterns, and so on—The Great Pumpkin and Linus in the pumpkin patch give us the kinder themes of generosity and hope bordering on faith in a higher being.

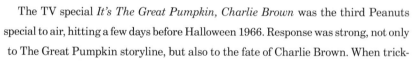

The TV special *It's The Great Pumpkin, Charlie Brown* was the third Peanuts special to air, hitting a few days before Halloween 1966. Response was strong, not only to The Great Pumpkin storyline, but also to the fate of Charlie Brown. When trick-or-treating, house after house gave him not candy, not an apple, not any sort of treat . . . but a rock. Years later, producer Lee Mendelson would note that every time that show ran, fans would send candy to Schulz's studio intended for poor Charlie Brown.

THIS PAGE: (top left) A partially inked seasonal sketch; (center left) animation cel from *It's The Great Pumpkin, Charlie Brown!*, which first aired in 1966; (bottom left) the special rendered in figurine form; (bottom right) a Halloween-themed strip. **OPPOSITE PAGE:** (top left) The Great Pumpkin visits MIT in 1962, courtesy of an impressive student prank; (top right) *Peanuts Projects*, an activity book published in 1963, featured this short three-act play; (bottom right) another production cel from the 1966 special.

ENCLOSURE: Cover and selected pages from *The Peanuts Book of Pumpkin Carols*, ca 1967. (on pouch) Layer of a cel presumably created for *It's The Great Pumpkin, Charlie Brown!*

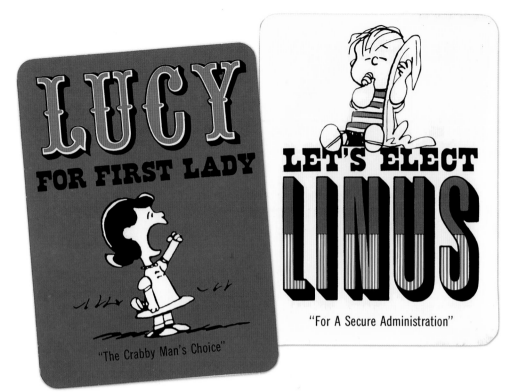

"The Crabby Man's Choice"

LET'S ELECT LINUS

"For A Secure Administration"

Peanuts characters, and his devotion to understanding and sharing his knowledge of The Great Pumpkin is unflagging. In a way, his faith may reflect his need for security, as seen by his carrying a comforting square of blue flannel that he must protect from Lucy and his blanket-hating grandma (both of who seem to want to separate him from the item for his own good), and from Snoopy (inviting the thrill of the chase). Indeed, protecting the blanket is a major source of insecurity in Linus's life, but who can blame him for wanting to safeguard such a versatile tool? Over the run of the strip, the blanket was used variously as a kite, a whip, a stuffed animal, a bindle sack, and the material for a storytelling flannelgraph.

Linus's blanket has taken on a life beyond the strip as well. Besides helping to popularize the term "security blanket," now used to refer to anything that comforts an individual, it has inspired many very real blankets: The organization Project Linus (officially unaffiliated with Schulz and Peanuts but clearly drawing inspiration from them) was founded in the mid-1990s to provide handmade blankets for ill or traumatized children. The charity has grown to foster the creation and delivery of over three million blankets.

Lucy & Linus

Neither Lucy nor Linus Van Pelt was part of the original Peanuts crew, although they both joined the strip early on. Each was introduced in 1952 as the basis for jokes about very young children, with Lucy appearing early in the year as an oddly goggle-eyed toddler and Linus appearing late in the year as a baby. They both grew up quickly while settling into their most important role: siblings. By the mid-1950s, they were the center of the strip's energy. Lucy played the loud, dominant older sister who sometimes showed her love for her younger brother by teaching him (usually with misinformation) and expressed her scorn by bullying him around. Though younger and physically weaker, Linus grew to be the smarter sibling, trying but unable to conquer with logic what Lucy complicated by sheer force of will.

Neither character is solely defined by their relationship to the other. Lucy wears her forceful personality like a badge. She's an ardent feminist who clearly believes in no woman more than herself. She is quick to suggest that the world bend itself to her vision, and her homemade psychiatric stand seems to serve that purpose while generating an income, however modest.

Linus, in contrast, is introverted, spiritual, and contemplative. He's also much quicker to recognize faults in himself. In his younger days, he bordered on magical, able to blow up a half-balloon and even a cubical balloon. Through the late 1950s and 1960s, he was a prodigy, playing outstanding outfield and erecting impressive houses of cards and sand sculptures. His Bible knowledge far surpassed that of the other

1950s 1960s 1970s 1980s 1990s

THIS PAGE: (top left) Campaign postcards, ca 1972; (top right and bottom left) Lucy and Linus "nodder" dolls featuring spring-mounted heads, ca 1976 and 1959, respectively. OPPOSITE PAGE: (top left) Sunday strip from March 4, 1956 and (top right) a draft sketch thought to be for its last panel; (bottom center) Lucy stars in this language guide, published in Japan; (bottom right) a fan letter from another very famous Lucy.

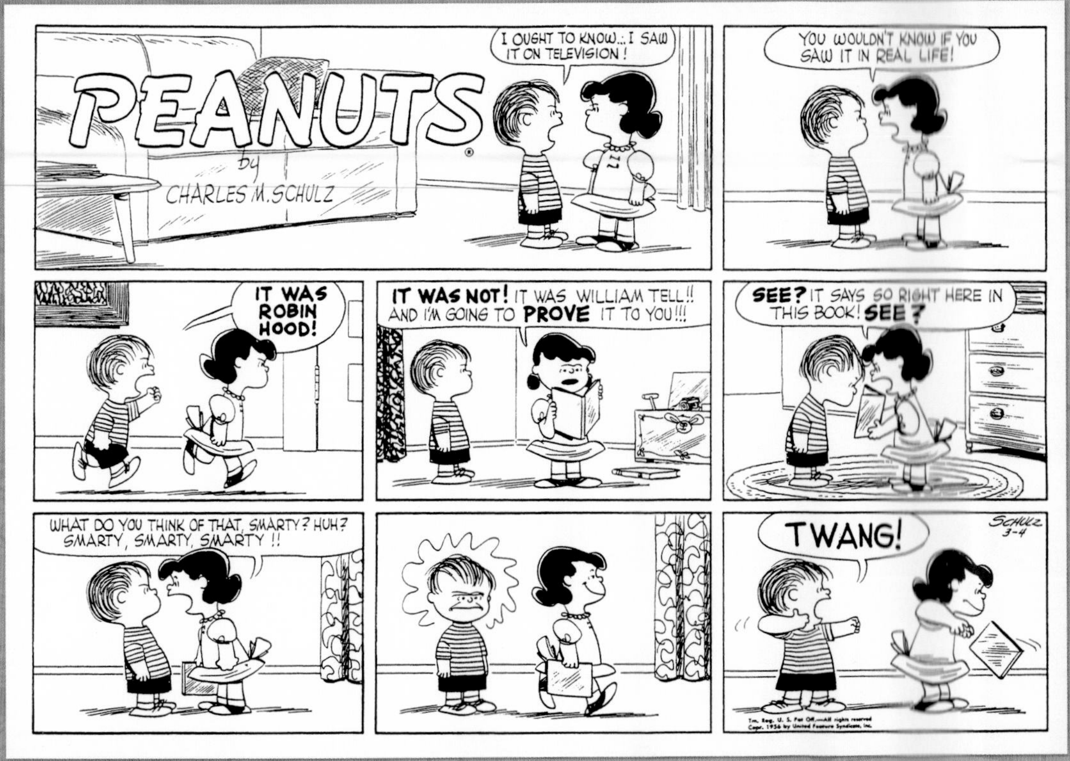
PEANUTS
by
CHARLES M. SCHULZ
I OUGHT TO KNOW... I SAW IT ON TELEVISION!
YOU WOULDN'T KNOW IF YOU SAW IT IN REAL LIFE!
IT WAS ROBIN HOOD!
IT WAS NOT! IT WAS WILLIAM TELL!! AND I'M GOING TO PROVE IT TO YOU!!!
SEE? IT SAYS SO RIGHT HERE IN THIS BOOK! SEE?
WHAT DO YOU THINK OF THAT, SMARTY? HUH? SMARTY, SMARTY, SMARTY!!
TWANG!
SCHULZ 3-4

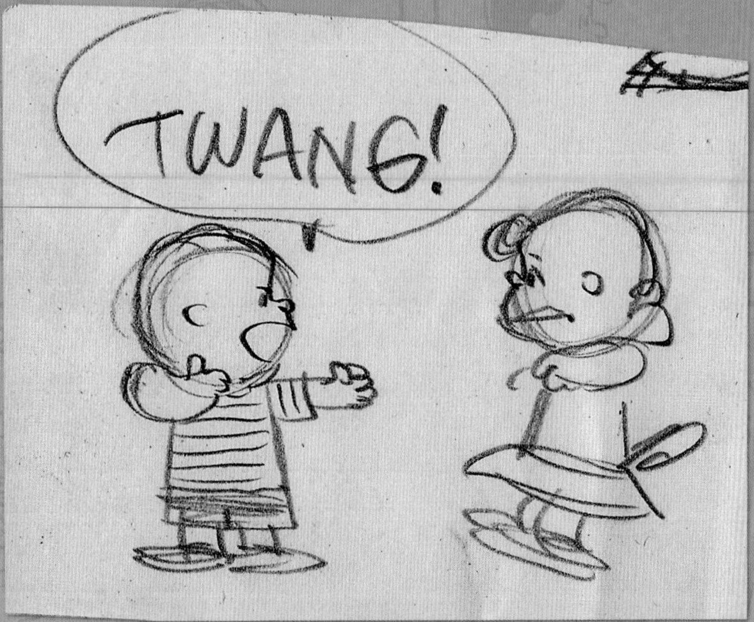
TWANG!

FEATURED: (bottom left) In 2006, Urban Outfitters created a cuddly real-life version of Linus's blanket. A portion of the proceeds goes to Project Linus.

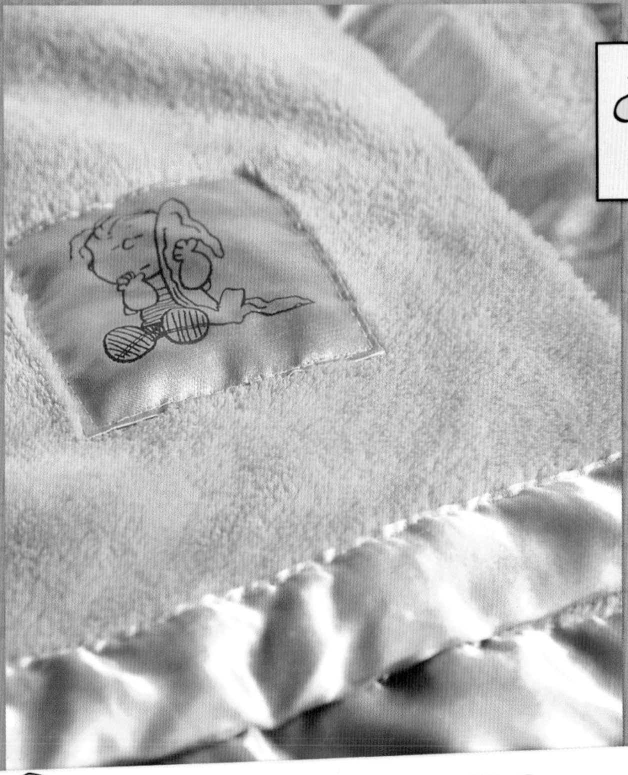

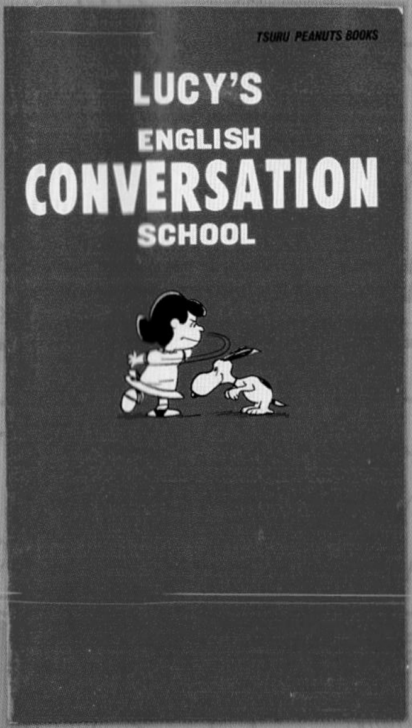
TSURU PEANUTS BOOKS
LUCY'S
ENGLISH
CONVERSATION
SCHOOL

Project ♥ Linus
Providing Security Through Blankets
© UFS

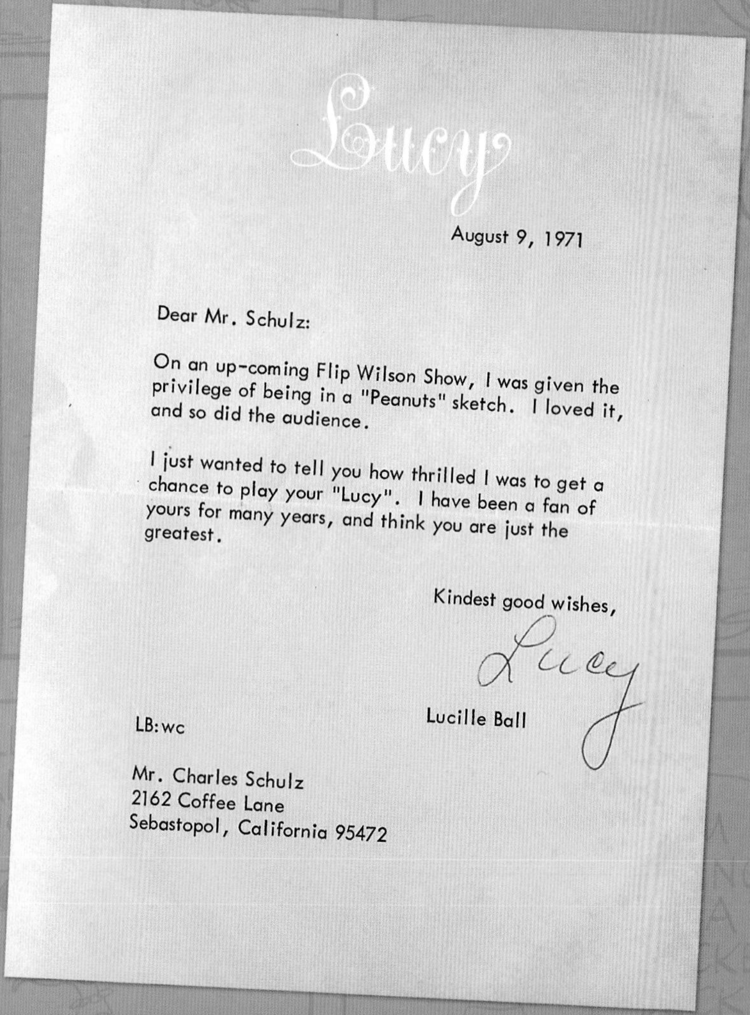

Lucy

August 9, 1971

Dear Mr. Schulz:

On an up-coming Flip Wilson Show, I was given the privilege of being in a "Peanuts" sketch. I loved it, and so did the audience.

I just wanted to tell you how thrilled I was to get a chance to play your "Lucy". I have been a fan of yours for many years, and think you are just the greatest.

Kindest good wishes,

Lucy

Lucille Ball

LB:wc

Mr. Charles Schulz
2162 Coffee Lane
Sebastopol, California 95472

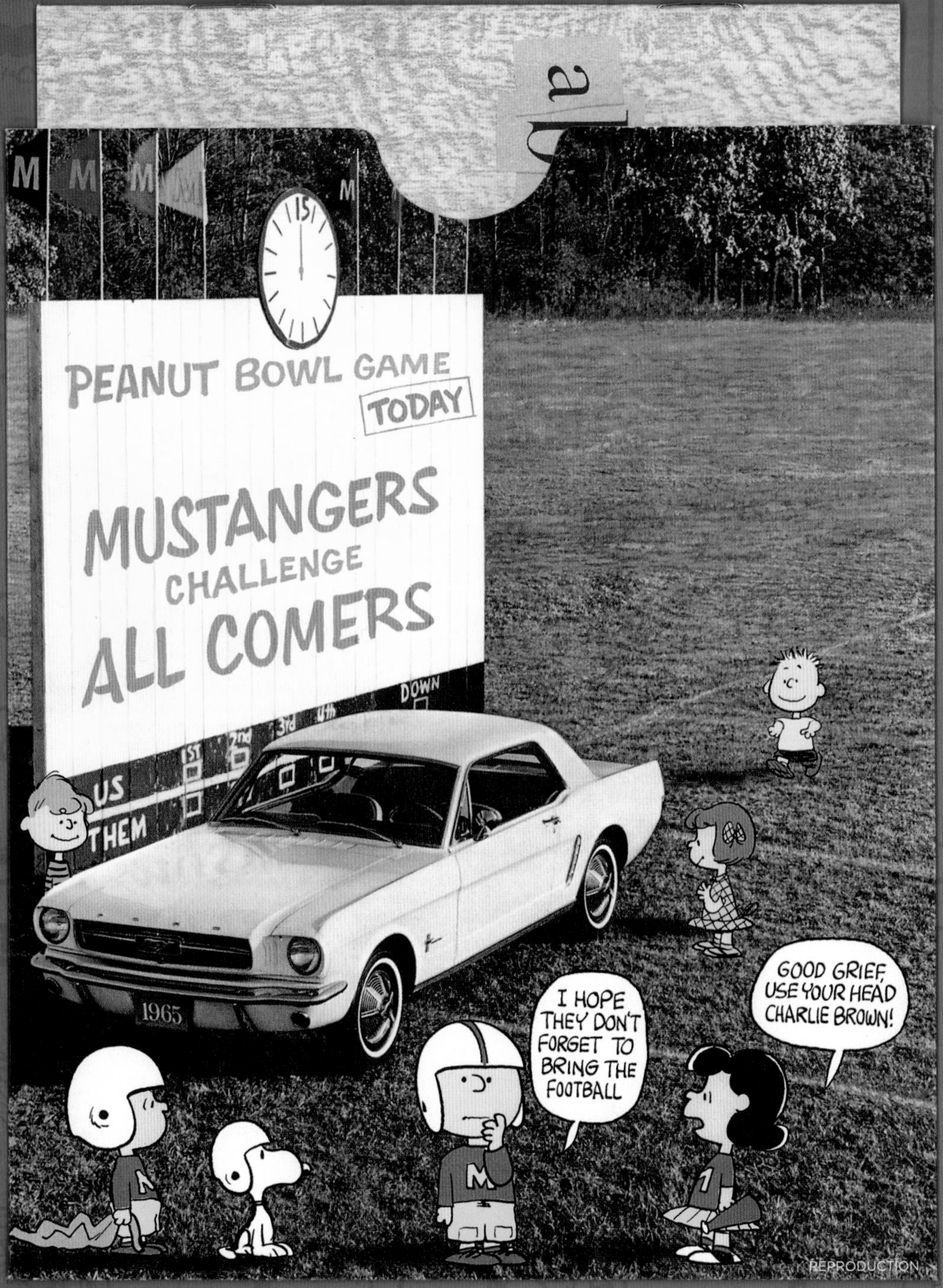
PEANUT BOWL GAME
TODAY
MUSTANGERS
CHALLENGE
ALL COMERS
DOWN
1ST 2ND 3RD 4TH
US
THEM
1965
I HOPE THEY DON'T FORGET TO BRING THE FOOTBALL
GOOD GRIEF, USE YOUR HEAD CHARLIE BROWN!
REPRODUCTION

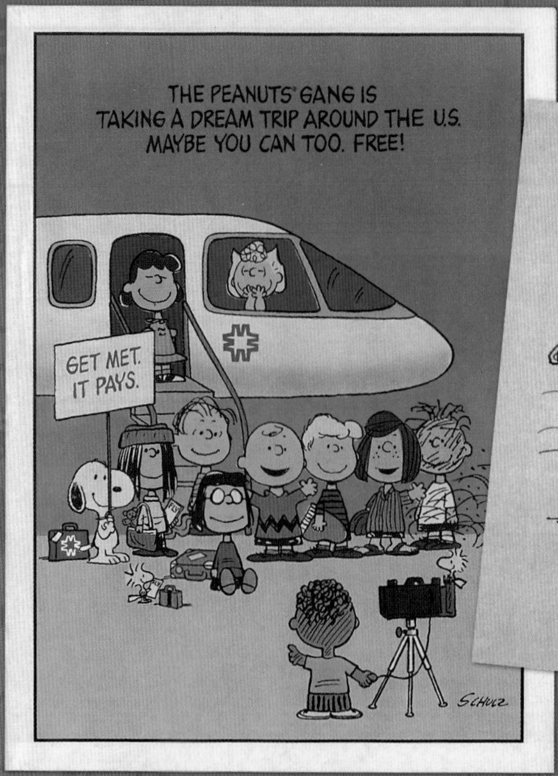
THE PEANUTS® GANG IS TAKING A DREAM TRIP AROUND THE U.S. MAYBE YOU CAN TOO. FREE!
GET MET. IT PAYS.
SCHULZ

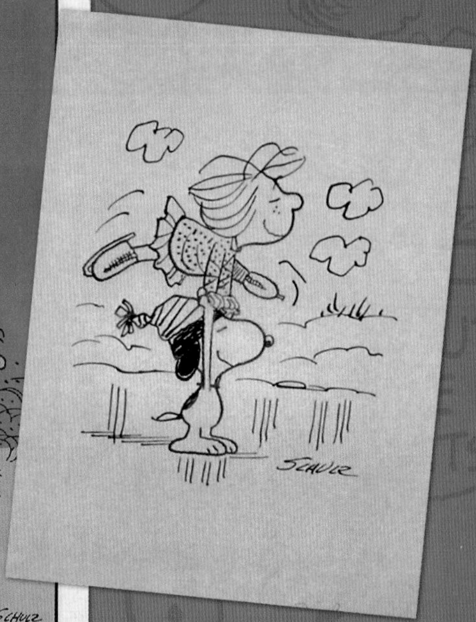
SCHULZ

ENCLOSURE: Selected pages from the "Scrapbook" manual that came standard with new Falcons in the 1960s. (on pouch) Schulz's team prepares to challenge "All Comers" on this brochure for the 1965 Ford Mustang.

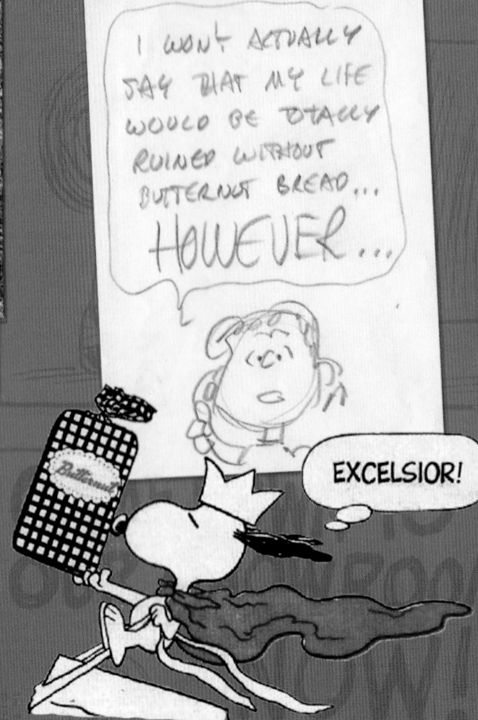
I WON'T ACTUALLY SAY THAT MY LIFE WOULD BE TOTALLY RUINED WITHOUT BUTTERNUT BREAD... HOWEVER...
Butternut
EXCELSIOR!

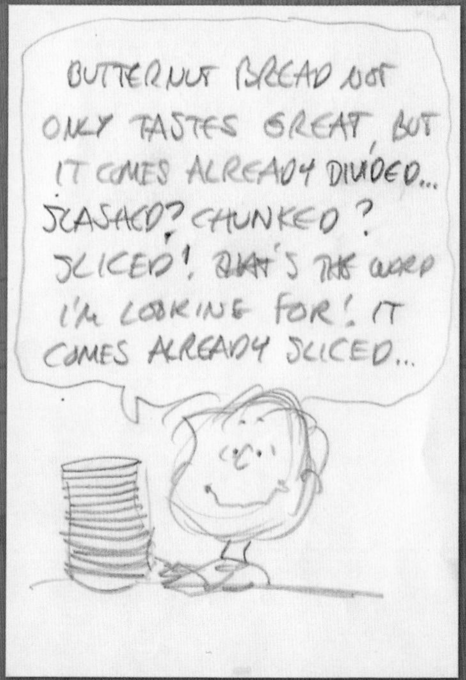
BUTTERNUT BREAD NOT ONLY TASTES GREAT, BUT IT COMES ALREADY DIVIDED...
CHUNKED? SLICED! THAT'S THE WORD I'M LOOKING FOR! IT COMES ALREADY SLICED...

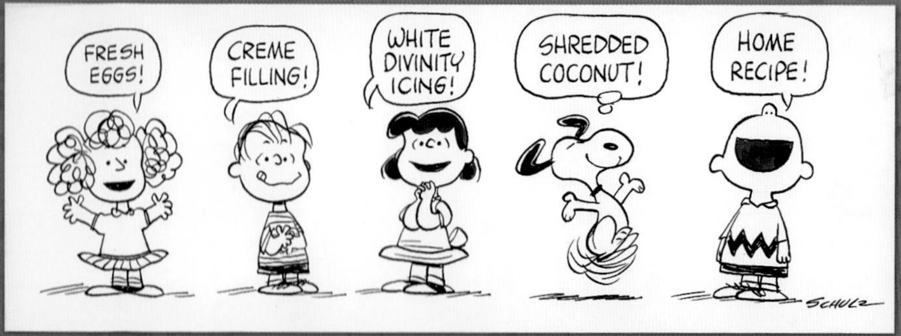
FRESH EGGS!
CREME FILLING!
WHITE DIVINITY ICING!
SHREDDED COCONUT!
HOME RECIPE!
SCHULZ

Advertising

The Peanuts crew has been used to advertise a wide range of products, from food to vacuum cleaners to insurance. Notably, these young characters have generally not been used to advertise to viewers their age—rather, they are used to reach an adult audience that cares about kids.

The Peanuts' first foray into advertising was a big one: Legendary agency J. Walter Thompson hired Charlie Brown and friends to act as spokespersons (and spokesdog) for the Falcon, then a new Ford model being pitched as an affordable family car. The campaign lasted for years and was multipronged, to say the least: Spots were created for television, animating the characters for the first time; magazine ads featured new Falcon-themed strips drawn by Schulz himself; auto showrooms were stocked with brochures starring the characters; and people who actually bought a car received a booklet on Falcon ownership filled with Peanuts artwork.

In the 1970s and 1980s, the characters' most visible place in advertising was promoting Dolly Madison snack cakes. The bakery was a prime sponsor of the animated specials, and they featured pictures of the Peanuts characters on their pies, donuts, and a range of small cake products with names like "Googles," "KooKoos," "Razzys," and "Zingers."

Both the Ford and Dolly Madison campaigns have been dwarfed, however, by the MetLife/Peanuts relationship, which has endured for a quarter century. "We've received a little bit of criticism for doing the insurance ads," Schulz noted in a 1988 interview with Michael Barrier. "A lot of people apparently don't believe in insurance." But the effect of Peanuts' role in the campaign has been positive; the link makes sense for the company's core life insurance business, especially if one considers that policy sales are driven largely by adults' concern for their children's well being.

At times, advertising has served Peanuts as more than just a source of revenue or exposure; it's actually helped expand the strip's borders to include new media. Bill Melendez, the animator who brought the characters to life for decades, first came aboard to animate the Ford ads. And the Peanuts animated TV specials may never have started if not for another advertiser, Coca-Cola, who specifically asked for a Peanuts program they could sponsor. Advertising has served Peanuts well . . . and judging by the length of some of the campaigns, Peanuts has served the advertisers well in return.

Charles Schulz . . .

Born in Minneapolis 27 years ago. Art Instruction correspondence course and night sketching classes at Minneapolis School of Art. Saw action as light-machine-gun squad leader in France and Germany during World War II. After war, became successful Saturday Evening Post contributor, instructor at Art Instruction, Inc., and cartoonist for St. Paul Pioneer Press, where Peanuts was created. His Post cartoons have been reprinted in the U. S. and many foreign countries.

UNITED FEATURES

PEANUTS
by SCHULZ

WATCH OUT FOR CHILDREN

The GREATEST little Sensation Since TOM THUMB!

OPPOSITE PAGE: (top right) Snoopy and Peppermint Patty skate through artwork for a MetLife campaign, ca 1986; (bottom left) Peanuts characters call out ingredients in Dolly Madison products; (bottom center and right) during the '70s, Snoopy, Lucy, and Linus champion Butternut Bread. **THIS PAGE:** (center right) Brochure created by United Feature Syndicate in 1950 to promote their new acquisition; (bottom right) these trading cards were distributed by MetLife.

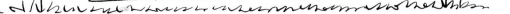

1950s 1960s 1970s 1980s 1990s

Snoopy

When Snoopy started out, he was a dog. Not a World War I flying ace, not a skating coach, not a Beagle Scout (nor a beagle, for that matter—more than a decade passed before he was accused of being a beagle, and even then he denied it). Schulz had wanted to name the big-nosed critter "Sniffy," but was dissuaded when he learned of another cartoon dog by that name; he fell back on a suggestion his mother once offered for the family dog.

Initially, Snoopy didn't even have visible thoughts; he was just the neighborhood pup. He jumped around, did basic dog tricks, chased balls, and hectored anyone who might have food. There was little consideration that he might become anything but a somewhat larger dog. But as time passed, his role expanded. He began to have dreams and thoughts; he "took on a personality that was very different from that of any previous cartoon dog," Schulz explained in *Peanuts Jubilee*. "He was slightly superior to the kids in the strip, although he did suffer a few defeats; you might say, at his own paws. But most of the time he won out over the kids."

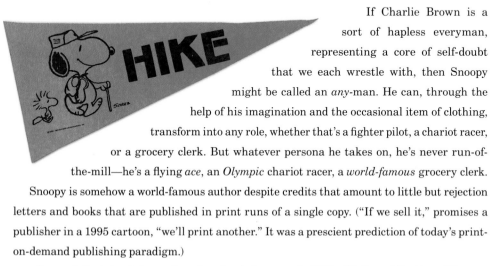

If Charlie Brown is a sort of hapless everyman, representing a core of self-doubt that we each wrestle with, then Snoopy might be called an *any*-man. He can, through the help of his imagination and the occasional item of clothing, transform into any role, whether that's a fighter pilot, a chariot racer, or a grocery clerk. But whatever persona he takes on, he's never run-of-the-mill—he's a flying *ace*, an *Olympic* chariot racer, a *world-famous* grocery clerk. Snoopy is somehow a world-famous author despite credits that amount to little but rejection letters and books that are published in print runs of a single copy. ("If we sell it," promises a publisher in a 1995 cartoon, "we'll print another." It was a prescient prediction of today's print-on-demand publishing paradigm.)

Snoopy's first step to becoming a breakout star came in 1958 with the publication of *Snoopy*, the first collection to focus on the antics of a single character. Toward the end of the book are strips in which Snoopy imitates a penguin, walking around on his hind feet. This capability made him all the more qualified to stand in for humans. It would have been tough for him to be Joe Cool, the Mad Punter, an ice skater, or any of myriad identities without walking upright (though

four-legged dog posture didn't prevent him from joining the softball team).

In 1967, Snoopy started hanging out with a small, fluffy yellow "bird hippy," a character that was destined to become his companion, secretary, and "friend of friends." Intelligible only to Snoopy and fellow birds, the little guy would remain nameless until June 22, 1970, when it was revealed that his name was Woodstock. Using the name of the music festival that had caused such a stir the year prior seemed appropriate, especially since the event had featured a little bird in its logo.

With Woodstock by his side, Snoopy grew to be a leader—of dogs (he was briefly Head Beagle), birds (as the scoutmaster of an otherwise all-bird Beagle Scout Troop), and humans (others began buying into his fantasies, which had previously made sense only to him). In a way his growth followed a very human trajectory—starting on all fours, learning to think in words, to stand and walk, to make friends, and ultimately to become a leader. Perhaps that's the reason it's possible to see ourselves in this little cartoon dog.

THIS PAGE: (center right) Two of enumerable publications starring the character; (bottom right) Joe Cool bares all in 1974. **OPPOSITE PAGE:** (top left) "Beagle Power" coaster; (top right) a sketch of Snoopy, ca 1970, with Amy Schulz's note to her dad at the top and to her fiance, ultimately the recipient, at the bottom; (center right); Snoopy works his magic in an original sketch.

BEAGLE POWER

SCHULZ

COPR. © UNITED FEATURE SYNDICATE, INC. 1958

DAD, This is a funny picture, you should use it.

I saw this piece of paper sitting by Dad's drawing board so I wrote that & Dad said I should mail this to you.

Snoopy's First Code Book

Charles M. Schulz
Kathryn W. Lumley

REPRODUCTION

ATTACHED: *Snoopy's First Code Book*, published in 1971, featured the eponymous character walking young readers through a series of brain puzzles.

Getting Animated

When animator-director Bill Melendez first set out to animate the characters for a series of Ford ads, he realized that Schulz hadn't designed the characters for three dimensions. They were recognizable from the front or side, but the angles in between were unclear. Schulz himself used the example that "with his large head and short arms, it would be very difficult to draw Linus sucking his thumb from the side, for he would have a hard time stretching out his arm that far . . . there are some poses that simply have to be avoided."

In 1963, producer Lee Mendelson tapped Melendez to animate Peanuts strips for a TV documentary he was making about Schulz. Schulz and Mendelson agreed on jazz composer/pianist Vince Guaraldi to provide the music. While the documentary never aired, the Schulz/Mendelson/Melendez/Guaraldi team was now in place. In 1965, they put together *A Charlie Brown Christmas* for CBS, which earned huge ratings and started a blockbuster television run. The team went on to produce about one special a year.

By 1969, Peanuts was too big to be contained by the small TV screen. The film *A Boy Named Charlie* shows Charlie Brown being his typical self, failing on all fronts. That all turns around when a pep talk and some advice from friends help him win the school spelling bee, earning him a place in the national championships. Charlie Brown becomes a hard-training, positive-thinking, spelling machine . . . only to lose the contest by misspelling "beagle," of all words.

"Much of the TV scripts incorporated material from the strip, along with the original material we developed," explains Mendelson. "It was an even bigger jump to a seventy-five-minute movie where it was over ninety percent original material. But we basically followed the same things that we used on the TV shows, from the kids' voices to the music to the artwork." The formula worked: *A Boy Named Charlie Brown*, which premiered at Radio City Music Hall, earned both critical acclaim and enough money to launch a series of films.

Their fourth and final cinematic outing, 1980's *Bon Voyage Charlie Brown (and Don't Come Back!)*, took Charlie Brown and friends into a mystery surrounding Chateau du Mal Voisin, a French manor that Schulz designed based on his housing during service in World War II. The European trip continues in the 1983 television special *What Have We Learned, Charlie Brown?*

Also in 1983, *The Charlie Brown and Snoopy Show* joined CBS's Saturday morning lineup of kids' TV. Eventually, CBS lost interest in new material (1994's *You're in the Super Bowl,*

Charlie Brown was their last new special); original cartoons were offered for home video, while the holiday classics continued to rerun.

In 2000, ABC acquired the broadcast rights and restored *A Charlie Brown Christmas* to its full running length. ABC also aired new specials, starting with 2002's *A Charlie Brown Valentine*. These specials used story lines taken directly from the strip. The most recent TV adventure, *He's a Bully, Charlie Brown*, was one Schulz himself had worked on before his passing. In it, Rerun Van Pelt loses his marbles (literally) to a marble shark (figurative). Charlie Brown gets Rerun's marbles back through a display of amazing marble skills—and the round-headed kid gets to end the special as both a winner and a hero.

THIS PAGE: (center left) A drawing for the cover of the Oct. 28, 1972, issue of *TV Guide*; (top right) Melendez at his desk with works in progress; (bottom right) black & white frames from *Race for Your Life, Charlie Brown!* (1977). **OPPOSITE PAGE:** (left) Poster promoting the first feature-length Peanuts movie; (top center) a production cel from *It's The Great Pumpkin, Charlie Brown!*; (top right) cel from the television special *What Have We Learned, Charlie Brown?* (1983).

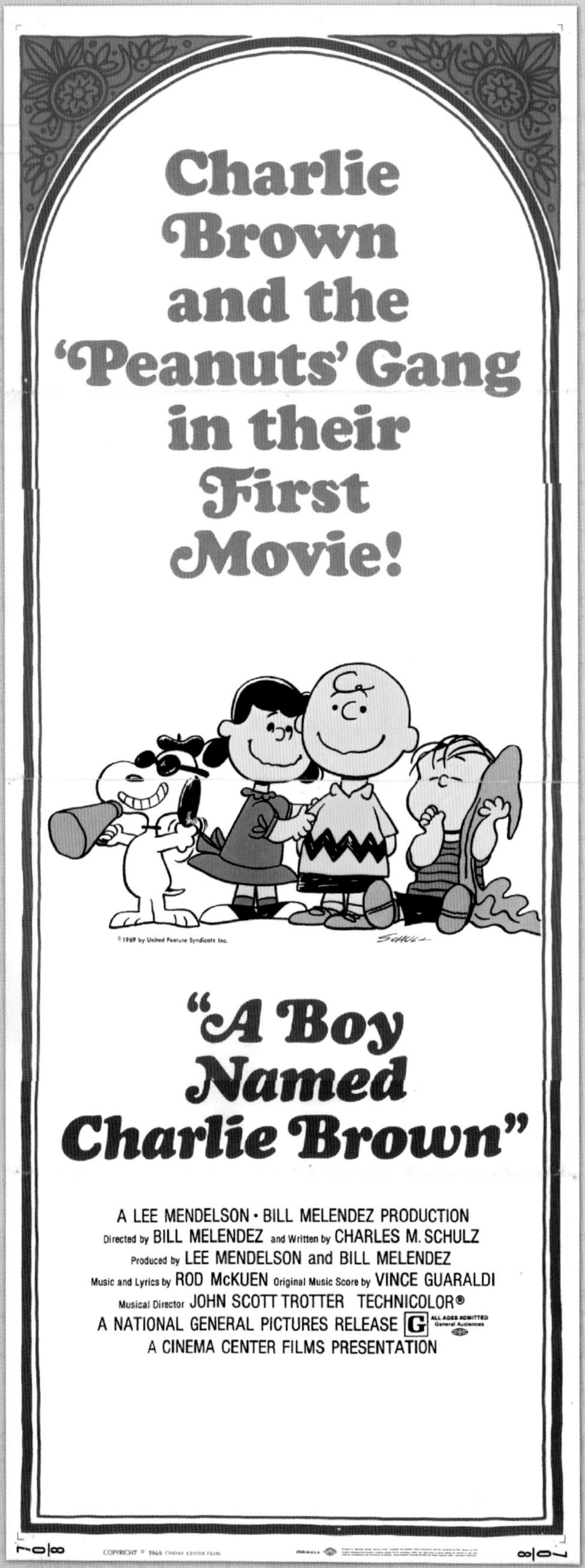

Charlie Brown and the 'Peanuts' Gang in their First Movie!
"A Boy Named Charlie Brown"
A LEE MENDELSON • BILL MELENDEZ PRODUCTION
Directed by BILL MELENDEZ and Written by CHARLES M. SCHULZ
Produced by LEE MENDELSON and BILL MELENDEZ
Music and Lyrics by ROD McKUEN Original Music Score by VINCE GUARALDI
Musical Director JOHN SCOTT TROTTER TECHNICOLOR®
A NATIONAL GENERAL PICTURES RELEASE G ALL AGES ADMITTED General Audiences
A CINEMA CENTER FILMS PRESENTATION
70/8

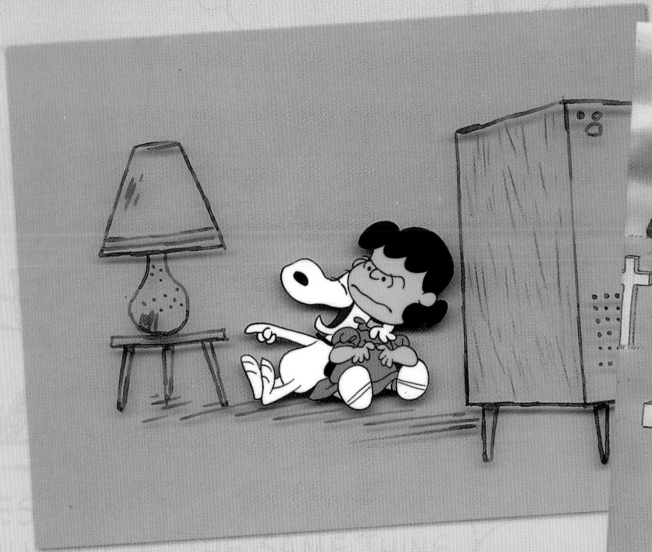

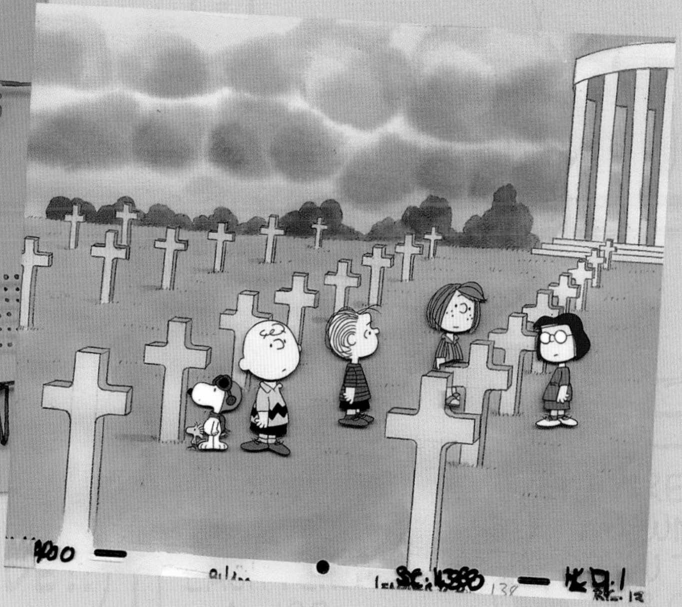

ENCLOSURE: A cel from the iconic dinner in *A Charlie Brown Thanksgiving*, first aired in 1973; (on pouch) a storyboard for *Snoopy Come Home* (1972).

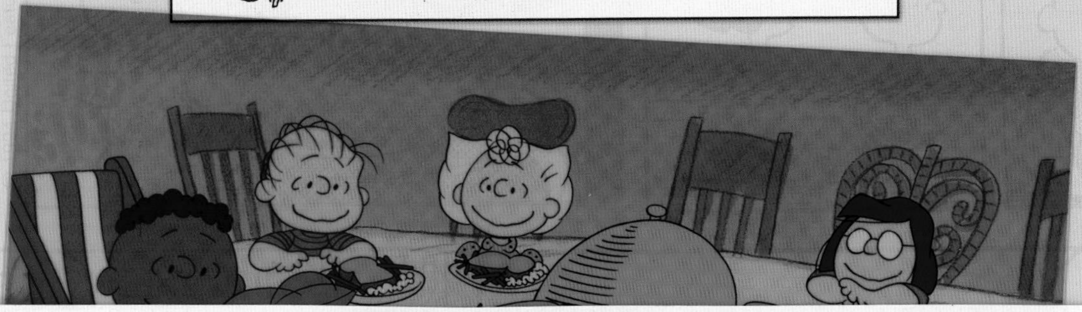

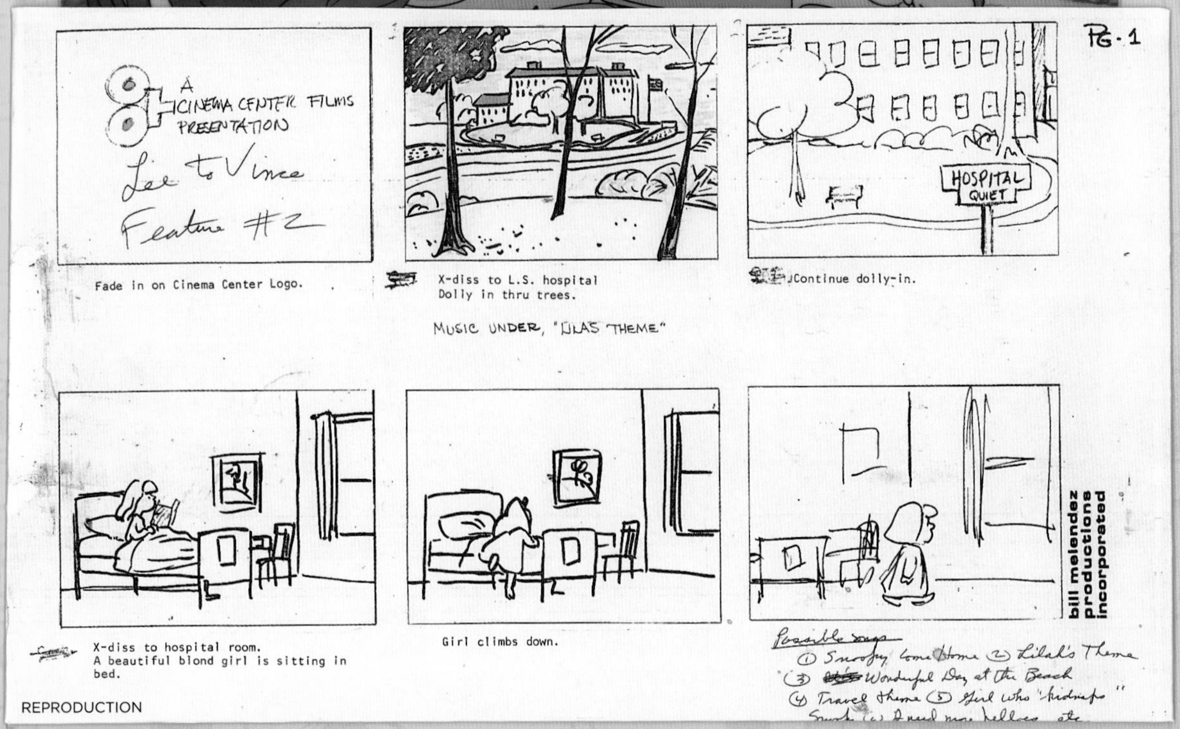

PG-1
A CINEMA CENTER FILMS PRESENTATION
Lee to Vince
Feature #2
Fade in on Cinema Center Logo.
X-diss to L.S. hospital
Dolly in thru trees.
HOSPITAL QUIET
Continue dolly-in.
MUSIC UNDER, "LILA'S THEME"
X-diss to hospital room.
A beautiful blond girl is sitting in bed.
Girl climbs down.
bill melendez productions incorporated
Possible songs
① Snoopy Come Home ② Lilah's Theme
③ Wonderful Day at the Beach
④ Travel theme ⑤ Girl who "kidnaps"
REPRODUCTION

Christmas

There has always been a place in Peanuts for Christmas. The first explicitly Christmas-themed strips appeared in 1951. The 1961 holiday season marked the first appearance of Peanuts Christmas cards, and the bestseller lists in 1964 featured the original Peanuts book, *Christmas is Together-Time*.

But it was in 1965 that it became clear *Christmas* had a place for Peanuts. That was the year when the Coca-Cola Company underwrote the creation of the very first Peanuts animated special, *A Charlie Brown Christmas*. More than fifteen million TVs were tuned in to that first broadcast, and the show has aired at least once every year since. By now many of those who viewed it the first time have grandkids to watch it with. After decades of being a tradition, it's easy to forget what a radical special it was, not just in its format (although its use of jazz music and real kid voices was groundbreaking for animated television), but also in its content. The story of people getting caught up in the trappings of the holiday, the decorations and pageantry, the glitter and the gifts, only to be reminded of what Christmas is truly about via a reading straight from the Bible, was not the safe path. Network television typically did not embrace such explicitly religious material.

The CBS network executives were famously unhappy with the special before it aired. (Even as the show was running dangerously close to deadline, the network was still arguing for the Bible passage to be cut and replaced.) They went ahead with airing it, not expecting great returns. But just as extra attention and decorations turned Charlie Brown's sad little Christmas tree into a thing of beauty, so did the huge ratings and critical acclaim transform the TV special in the eyes of its critics, who were glad to give the show an annual home (and order more Peanuts specials as well).

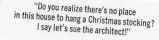

"Do you realize there's no place in this house to hang a Christmas stocking? I say let's sue the architect!"

A Charlie Brown Christmas was not afraid to look at the complexities and difficulties of Christmas, considerations that have always been embraced in the strip. Yes, Christmas was a time of celebration and even reflection, but Peanuts didn't shy from themes of greed and commercialization. It was a time when celebrating could mean the terrifying pressure placed on children performing in a pageant, and the days after the holiday might be filled with writing thank-you notes for presents that had already broken. And as with so much of Peanuts, we can see our lives, our stresses, and our fears reflected in what happens to the characters, making it easier to welcome the stories into our hearts and homes.

The place for Peanuts in Christmas has grown since that time. There are three more animated Christmas specials, and a huge array of ornaments and decorations. Peanuts is part of the visual language of Christmas, and that's thanks to the special tale of one young boy who believed in the plainest of Christmas trees, and an even younger boy with a surprisingly strong memory for the Gospel. That's the show that won the Emmy award, the Peabody award, and a place in the hearts of millions.

THIS PAGE: (top left) Animation cel from *A Charlie Brown Christmas* (1965); (center) classic Peanuts ornaments; (top right) a sketch for "Charlie Brown's Christmas Stocking," a feature in *Good Housekeeping* magazine, Dec. 1963. OPPOSITE PAGE: (top left) The crew in ornament form; (bottom center) Peanuts snow globe; (bottom right) album cover to the animated special's soundtrack.

ENCLOSURE: Schulz designed this card especially for actor Roy Casstevens (who played Schroeder in the 1967–72 San Francisco production of *You're a Good Man, Charlie Brown*) and allowed him to print about 100 for personal use.

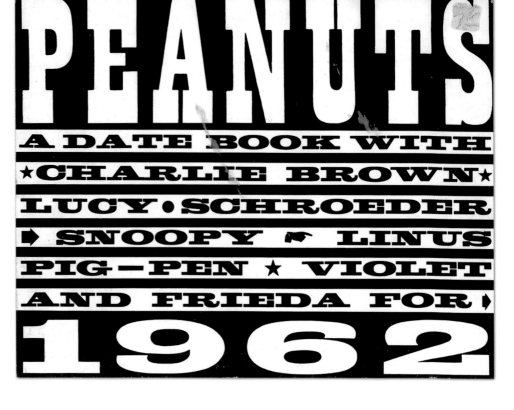

Peanuts Everywhere

In the beginning, Schulz wasn't really interested in seeing Peanuts merchandise. He certainly understood that a popular comic strip could have licensing opportunities—as a kid, he'd seen Popeye bounce off of the comics page and onto products. Just a year before United Feature Syndicate brought the first Peanuts strips to newspapers, their *Li'l Abner* strip had a huge public hit with its Shmoo characters, spawning watches and wallpapers, ties and games, and just about anything else one could adorn with a cuddly little blob. But Schulz's dreams were of cartooning, not of marketing. "He didn't want any merchandising at all," explains Dale Hale, an artist who worked in Schulz's studio in the 1950s.

Schulz remained a reluctant licensing partner even after Hungerford produced the first dolls in the late 1950s. When it came to licensing, "He'd say, 'I'm not gonna do that,'" Hale recalls. But eventually demand grew too strong to ignore and, says Hale, "That changed a lot." The success of each venture Schulz cooperated with lead to a desire from the public for more products. Additionally, Schulz was unhappy with some of what had appeared, feeling that the characters didn't look right when drawn by other artists; from an emotional perspective, he stood to benefit from more creative control. Ultimately, Schulz reached an agreement wherein he would cooperate with licensing as long as he had approval rights. And wherever possible, the licensed material would directly reproduce Schulz's art rather than new drawings.

THIS PAGE: (top left) A large program prescribing physical fitness; (top center) cookbook with recipes from noted female athletes; (top right) cover of Determined Productions' datebook. OPPOSITE PAGE: (top right) Helping to convey the *Fundamentals of Physics*; (center right) Tapioca Pudding's savvy commentary; (bottom left) edible Peanuts; (bottom center) words of wisdom; (bottom right) an oversized coloring book comprised of Sunday strip reprints.

Thus the floodgates were opened. Before 1960, there were just a handful of Peanuts items besides books and comic books. In 1960, Hallmark printed the first of what would turn out to be literally billions of greeting cards with the Peanuts characters. In 1961, Determined Productions produced its first Peanuts product, a datebook. This led to a line of Determined products featuring a distinct design sensibility, with bright, solid colors that served Schulz's clean lines well. In turn came a line of attractive items popular in the years leading up to the psychedelic era; the combination of near Day-Glo colors with philosophy coming out of the mouths of children suited the times. In the decade that followed, the Peanuts characters continued to enter new media; with each entry came more exposure, more popularity, and more products. Soon fans across Europe and Asia were smitten with Peanuts items, too.

Peanuts licensing continues to reach into almost every aspect of life, and every room of the house. A kitchen could have several Peanuts recipe books. The drawer may have Peanuts flatware, while the cupboards may hold Peanuts glasses and Peanuts plates. Those plates may be used to serve canned Peanuts pasta with meatballs, or waffles in the shape of Snoopy's head. The drink may be Snoopy's Sweet S'Mores Cocoa in a Peppermint Patty mug, and for dessert, Peanuts candies or fruit snacks.

All along, the strip remained pure, and would even poke fun at concepts that existed only for licensing's sake using Tapioca Pudding, a short-lived character who would gleefully and irritatingly talk about her own licensability. But Schulz became more comfortable with licensing on the whole. In an introduction to one of many Peanuts collectibles guidebooks, he admits, "We all like to have something as a reminder of characters that we follow every day in the newspapers."

THE SNOOPY DOGHOUSE COOK BOOK

59 RECIPES FOR YOUR DOG

BY EVELYN SHAW, PH.D.

15. A dog, weighing 10.0 lb is standing on a flatboat so that he is 20 ft from the shore. He walks 8.0 ft on the boat toward shore and then halts. The boat weighs 40 lb, and one can assume there is no friction between it and the water. How far is he from the shore at the end of this time? (*Hint:* The center of mass of boat + dog does not move. Why?) The shoreline is also to the left in Fig. 8–11.

FIGURE 8–11

Fundamentals of PHYSICS

David Halliday
Robert Resnick

HI! MY NAME IS TAPIOCA PUDDING

I KNOW

MY DAD IS IN LICENSING.. MY PICTURE IS GOING TO BE ON GREETING CARDS AND LUNCH BOXES

IF YOU WERE MY BOYFRIEND, YOU WOULDN'T HAVE TO CARRY MY PICTURE IN YOUR WALLET..

IT WOULD ALREADY BE ON YOUR LUNCH BOX!

I CAN'T STAND IT!

FEATURED: Cover and selected recipe from Snoopy's cookbook— certifiably beagle approved.

It's impossible to be gloomy when you're sitting behind a marshmallow...

THE COLORFUL WORLD OF SNOOPY LINUS SCHROEDER LUCY AND CHARLIE BROWN

COPR. © UNITED FEATURE SYNDICATE, INC. 1954

Keep America Clean

SCHULZ

To: Joan — with Best Wishes! Walt Handelsman 2003

WALT HANDELSMAN © 2003 Newsday

...AND MY REPLACEMENT FOR CHRISTIE TODD WHITMAN...

★ EPA ★

* APOLOGIES TO SCHULZ

FEATURED: (center) One of a series of bobbing-head figures created by the Danish Lego Company in 1959.

PIG PEN
OF THE PEANUTS COMIC STRIP

PEANUTS

IT'S FANTASTIC!

I'M PERFECTLY CLEAN NOW, BUT JUST LET ME STEP OUT OF THE HOUSE FOR ONE MINUTE...

WHAM!

YOU KNOW WHAT I AM? I'M A DUST MAGNET!

11-25

SCHULZ

Pig-Pen

When a cartoonist introduces a new character into an existing comic, the hope is that this character will bring a lot to the strip. And that's certainly true of Pig-Pen (or "Pigpen" or "Pig-Pen"—the punctuation changed repeatedly over the years). He brought the soil of ancient Babylon, the dust of ancient civilizations . . .

Pig-Pen's real name is—well, he doesn't have one. It's not just that he's never given one in the strip; in his very first appearance (July 13, 1954) he states specifically "I haven't got a name . . . people just call me things . . . real insulting things . . . " Forty-five years later, we do learn what people call his dad: "Pigpen, Senior."

Pig-Pen is not incapable of being clean, it's just a very temporary situation when he is. "I like to take baths," he confesses. "The whole trouble with me is that I like getting dirty even better!"

At first, Pig-Pen was merely dirty, perhaps raising a cloud of dust if he clapped. In 1957, he began being surrounded by a cloud of dust whenever he walked. In 1961, it became clear that he didn't even have to move; a miasma of dust was ever-present. In some ways, this was a great defining visual characteristic, but in other ways, it limited him as a character. Pig-Pen couldn't be just casually part of the gang in the strip, because the moment he was there, he grabbed all the visual attention. If he was in the strip for more than a panel, it had to be pretty much about him. "There is no reason for having him in the strip unless the idea has something to do with a kid who is always dirty," explained Schulz in the book *Charlie Brown, Snoopy, and Me*. "Usually, I just run out of ideas for him, but somehow he keeps hanging in there." Pig-Pen was notably absent from the strip for years at a time, and was rarely seen from the mid-1960s to 1980.

In 1980, however, Pig-Pen got something that Peanuts characters rarely get: a happy romantic involvement. Charlie Brown set him up on a date with a gal who is quite earthy in her own way: Peppermint Patty. They went to a Valentine's Day dance together, and over the next couple months, there were signs of mutual affection.

In terms of the number of strips he appeared in, Pig-Pen is a relatively minor character, but in terms of reader impact, he's sizable. People recognize him instantly and know what he's about. And while his unsanitary nature has kept him from joining the rest of the Peanuts crew in some of their ad appearances (somehow a Pig-Pen Snack Pie just doesn't sound yummy), he made a perfect spokesman for one product's campaign: Regina vacuum cleaners.

OPPOSITE PAGE: (top right) Matt Handelsman's nod to Schulz in a 2003 editorial cartoon for *Newsday*; (center right) partial Pig-Pen strip; (bottom) a rare (and fleeting) vision of the character clean. **THIS PAGE:** (top right) A recycling message that ran in *USA Today Weekend Magazine* in May 1989.

You're
in School
Now,
Charlie Brown
by
Charles M. Schulz

Snoopy's ABCs
Snoopy Counts to 10

In the Classroom

The Peanuts kids spent a lot of time in school, of course, with many strips to prove it. But that's not the only way they made it into the classroom.

The characters have been used repeatedly to teach English. The most notable such usage for native English speakers is the *Snoopy's Code Book* textbook series (see page 21). Launched in 1971, these books taught reading and writing using examples from Peanuts strips to show phonetic pronunciation of words. Advanced students in Europe had *School Peanuts*, a series written entirely in English and published in Denmark. Through a mix of strips and text, these books introduce readers to aspects of American culture as well as the English language. (Baseball, American television, and the notion of The Great Pumpkin all make appearances.) Japanese readers could learn using the *English Conversational School* books, where volumes of Peanuts strips as well as volumes of other popular American comic strips were used to teach English.

The Peanuts animation team got into the education game with *Charlie Brown's Career Education Program*, a series of filmstrips presenting still images and the full Peanuts voice cast. These thirty-five short tales, aimed at students from kindergarten through eighth grade,

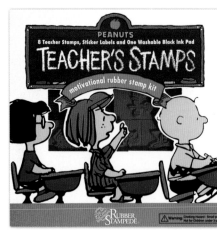

each carried a moral about finding a job that was personally satisfying. The series also created a job for the young voice actress behind Dolores, a Latina character created just for the films. Her presence, along with frequent appearances by Franklin, lent the cast more ethnic diversity.

Of course, education doesn't take place solely within the walls of the classroom, and in 1988, the Peanuts crew brought their educational power to televisions across the United States. *This is America, Charlie Brown* was the first-ever animated miniseries. Producer Lee Mendelson says that as proud as he is of the most famous Peanuts holiday specials, he is "equally proud of the eight-part mini-series." Each episode focused on a different aspect of U.S. history, introducing the gang to some of the greatest figures of the nation's past. (Apparently if you're a founding father, a great inventor, or someone of a similar stature, you're allowed to be an exception to the "no adults in Peanuts" rule.)

THIS PAGE: (top left) Animation cel from *This is America, Charlie Brown*; (top right and center) three of many educational publications. **OPPOSITE PAGE:** (top center) Peanuts share lessons across geographical and language boundaries; (bottom right) Snoopy the master student—and wastebasket star.

EDUCATORS
AT WORK

schoolhouse [ˈskuːlhaus; sk: lhaus]名校舍.
Charlie Brown is running out of the **schoolhouse**.
查理布朗從校舍跑了出來。
He's running away from the **building where he goes to
school.**
他從上學的建築物中跑開了。
School is over
for the day.
這一天的課上完了。

[three hundred and thirty-three] 333

SNOOPY

(美)布加塞·辞尔斯
SCHULZ

SNOOPY DICTIONARY
史努比
英汉辞典
中国工商出版社

THE VALUATOR

SPRING '69

I AM A GREAT
ADMIRER OF THE
MODERN SCHOOL
TEACHER!

Tm. Reg. U. S. Pat. Off.—All rights reserved
© 1969 by United Feature Syndicate, Inc.

THE AMERICAN ECONOMIC SYSTEM
AND YOUR PART IN IT

Gratefully presented to

CHARLES M. SCHULZ

in recognition of material contributions to the cause
of "economic literacy" through support of The Advertising
Council's American Economic System Campaign to encourage
greater public understanding of the American economic system.

FEATURED: (top right) Framed medal awarded to Schulz for
his contributions to "The American Economic System and [His]
Part in It."

I will not talk in class.
I will not talk in class.

I will not talk in class.
I will not talk in class.
I will not talk in class.

I will not talk in class.
I will not talk in class.
I will not talk in class.

On the other hand, who
knows what I'll do?

SCHULZ

THIS IS MY REPORT
ON WALTER DIEMER,
THE MAN WHO
INVENTED BUBBLE GUM..

OBVIOUSLY, WE
ARE ALL
GRATEFUL TO HIM..

AUDIO VISUAL,
MA'AM..

10-21

© 1996 United Feature Syndicate, Inc.

SCHULZ

DIPLOMA
R—
Jerry

CUM
LAUDE

SCHULZ

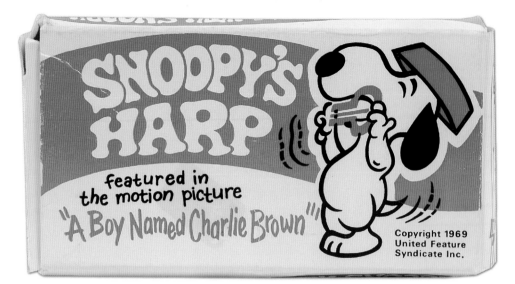

Music to Our Ears

The first notes to appear in the *Peanuts* strip were classical music—or meant to be, anyway. Before Schroeder arrived, Beethoven haunted poor Charlie Brown. Try as he might to coax Ludwig's works from his violin, he managed to produce only broken notes, causing him to fear the composer. Once Schroeder took to the task, however, well-played music became the rule.

When Peanuts music reached records and TV, it came in jazz form. Grammy winner Vince Guaraldi composed original music for a 1963 documentary about Schulz and his strip that was intended for TV but never aired. Nevertheless, a recording of the music was issued in 1964, titled *Jazz Impressions of a Boy Named Charlie Brown*, and it included the piece that would later be recognized as the Peanuts theme: a song called "Linus and Lucy." That tune and others finally reached TV in 1965 as part of *A Charlie Brown Christmas*, securing jazz as the Peanuts sound. Guaraldi continued to provide the music for the TV specials until his death in 1976 at age 47. His compositions were integrated into later TV offerings, some of which were scored and performed by respected jazz players such as David Benoit, George Winston, Dave Brubeck, and Wynton Marsalis.

A handful of these tunes became standard. Music lovers can download a variety of renditions of "Linus and Lucy" online, ranging from traditional jazz takes to steel drum reggae to a version sung by cats. Among the hundreds of acts who have recorded "Christmastime is Here" are Sarah McLachlan, Barry Manilow, Tony Bennett, Al Jarreau, Spyro Gyra, Chicago, Rosemary Clooney, and Mexican Elvis impersonator El Vez.

When Peanuts music really hit the radio hard, though, it wasn't classical or jazz, but pure, rockin' pop. In 1966, producer Phil Gernhard approached Florida-based garage band The Royal Guardsmen with some unlikely lyrics he wanted them to set to music and record. "Snoopy vs. the Red Baron" told of the air battles in which "a funny looking dog with a big black nose"

challenged the famed Baron von Richthofen. The folksy result of this collaboration, underscored by a marching drum line, captured the public's attention. The song reached as high as number 2 on the Billboard Hot 100 chart, and response from live audiences was enormous. "Some venues were so big you couldn't hear the cadence of the snare drum over the fans screaming," remembers The Royal Guardsmen drummer John Burdett.

Success breeds repetition, and the Guardsmen followed their hit with a series of songs in which Snoopy again faces down the Red Baron (if sometimes only implicitly). The band dissolved a few years after, only to reform decades later, again with Snoopy in tow. "In Vietnam, the soldiers liked listening to 'Snoopy vs. The Red Baron' and on a couple of aircraft carriers, the scramble alert was the beginning of the song," explains Burdett. "So, we thought we would write a song for today's soldiers," which they indeed did.

But it's Peanuts music from the 1960s that fills the airwaves and the malls' sound systems when Christmastime rolls around. Guaraldi's beloved "Linus and Lucy" and "Christmastime is Here" (a song from *A Charlie Brown Christmas* with lyrics by producer Lee Mendleson) bring warm thoughts to mind without the mention of a single character.

THIS PAGE: (top left) Snoopy's twangy metal mouth harp, as featured in *A Boy Named Charlie Brown*; (center) the stage show soundtrack; (top right) *The Electric Company* magazine, based around the PBS TV series. **OPPOSITE PAGE:** (top and center left) Album covers from The Royal Guardsmen and a musical soundtrack; (bottom center) Peanuts sheet music; (bottom right) an Italian strip collection's cover.

FEATURED: (top right) Album and record cover from a popular Vince Guaraldi Trio soundtrack.

© 1966 United Feature Syndicates, Inc.

FEATURED: (top left) *Playbill* and (attached, top right) program from the popular play, ca 1967.

Taking to the Stage

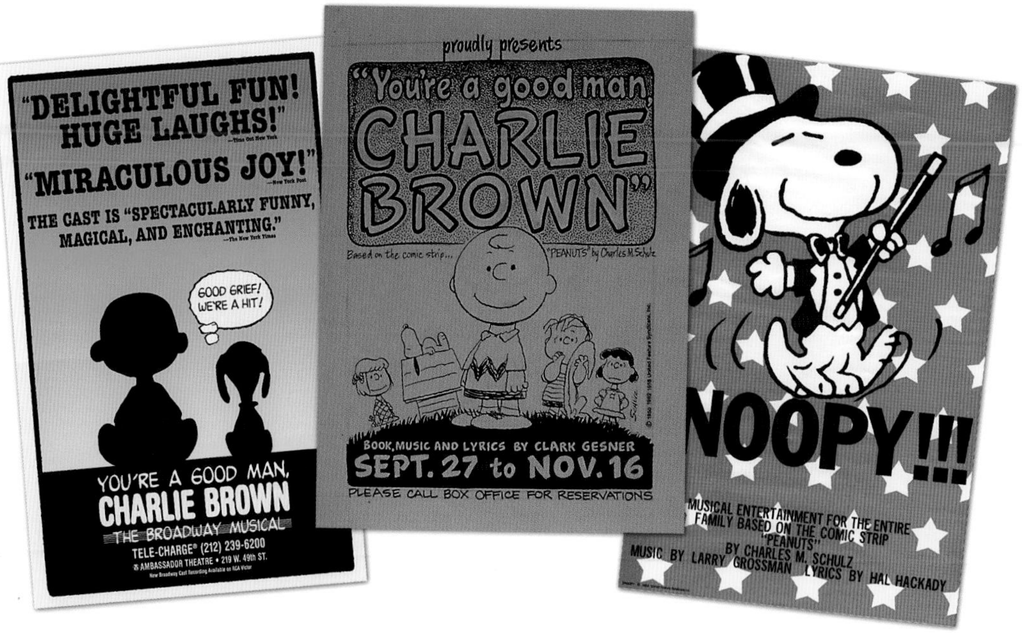

"DELIGHTFUL FUN! HUGE LAUGHS!"
"MIRACULOUS JOY!"
THE CAST IS "SPECTACULARLY FUNNY, MAGICAL, AND ENCHANTING."
GOOD GRIEF! WE'RE A HIT!
YOU'RE A GOOD MAN, CHARLIE BROWN
THE BROADWAY MUSICAL
TELE-CHARGE® (212) 239-6200
AMBASSADOR THEATRE • 219 W. 49th ST.
proudly presents
"You're a good man, CHARLIE BROWN"
Based on the comic strip... "PEANUTS" by Charles M. Schulz
BOOK, MUSIC AND LYRICS BY CLARK GESNER
SEPT. 27 to NOV. 16
PLEASE CALL BOX OFFICE FOR RESERVATIONS
NOOPY!!!
MUSICAL ENTERTAINMENT FOR THE ENTIRE FAMILY BASED ON THE COMIC STRIP "PEANUTS" BY CHARLES M. SCHULZ
MUSIC BY LARRY GROSSMAN LYRICS BY HAL HACKADY

The first Peanuts play was never performed on Broadway . . . or off-Broadway, or at any other commercial venue, for that matter. Rather, *The Great Pumpkin Mystery: A Stirring Play in Three Acts* was performed in living rooms, playrooms, and backyards. This play of three very short acts was published in 1963 in *Peanuts Projects*, an oversized activity book. (The storyline is based on the same strips that would inspire *It's the Great Pumpkin, Charlie Brown* a few years later.)

When Charlie Brown and friends did finally hit the stage, their impact was as big as their production values were modest. *You're a Good Man, Charlie Brown* features a cast of just six actors and a set comprised of a few simple, blocky shapes, making it easily staged in a small local theater, rather than requiring large-scale Broadway treatment. The play itself was not so much written as accumulated: built around a group of songs released on an earlier album, composed by the previously unknown Clark Gesner, the book for the play was credited to "John Gordon" (who didn't actually exist), but the production itself was workshopped by Gesner, the cast, and anyone else with ideas for integrating existing Peanuts strips into a coherent whole. The process benefitted from a strong base of raw talent, including musical director Joe Raposo, years before his memorable work on *Sesame Street*; Gary Burghoff, who embodied Charlie Brown long before he became *M*A*S*H*'s Radar O'Reilly; and Bob Balaban, the future Tony- and Oscar-nominated actor/director/producer who played Linus.

When the show launched at Theater 80 St. Marks in New York's East Village on March 7, 1967, there was still no actual written script; eventually, what the actors were performing was transcribed so that other actors could take it on. And take it on they did. The show quickly spread, with new casts forming across North America and beyond even as the original New York show continued, running just shy of 1,600 performances. In 1971, it landed on Broadway for the first time. Almost three decades and a slight rewrite later, *You're a Good Man, Charlie Brown* returned to Broadway in 1999 and earned its cast and crew multiple Tony Awards. Eventually made available for school and community theaters to produce, the show has been performed more often than any other musical in American history, and understandably so: It's easy to stage, the songs are charming, and its characters are instantly familiar.

A second Peanuts show, *Snoopy!!!: The Musical*, debuted in San Francisco in 1975. Even though it had little of the creative team as *You're a Good Man* (although it was still rooted in the work of Schulz, of course), it developed in much the same style, as a series of scenes, sketches, and songs rather than one long story. It was significantly expanded in the 1980s for a successful run in London.

In the 1980s, the stage musicals were adapted into animated TV specials, which proved just how mutable Peanuts can be. For example, when the characters sing "Happiness Is" at the end of TV's *You're a Good Man, Charlie Brown*, audiences are seeing an animated adaptation of a stage adaptation of an album presentation of a song that was based on a book (*Happiness is a Warm Puppy* was an original Peanuts book that spent most of 1963 on the bestseller list) based on a comic strip. (Phew!) That one song shows how Peanuts can conquer many media, but it all still traces back to the heart of Schulz's strip.

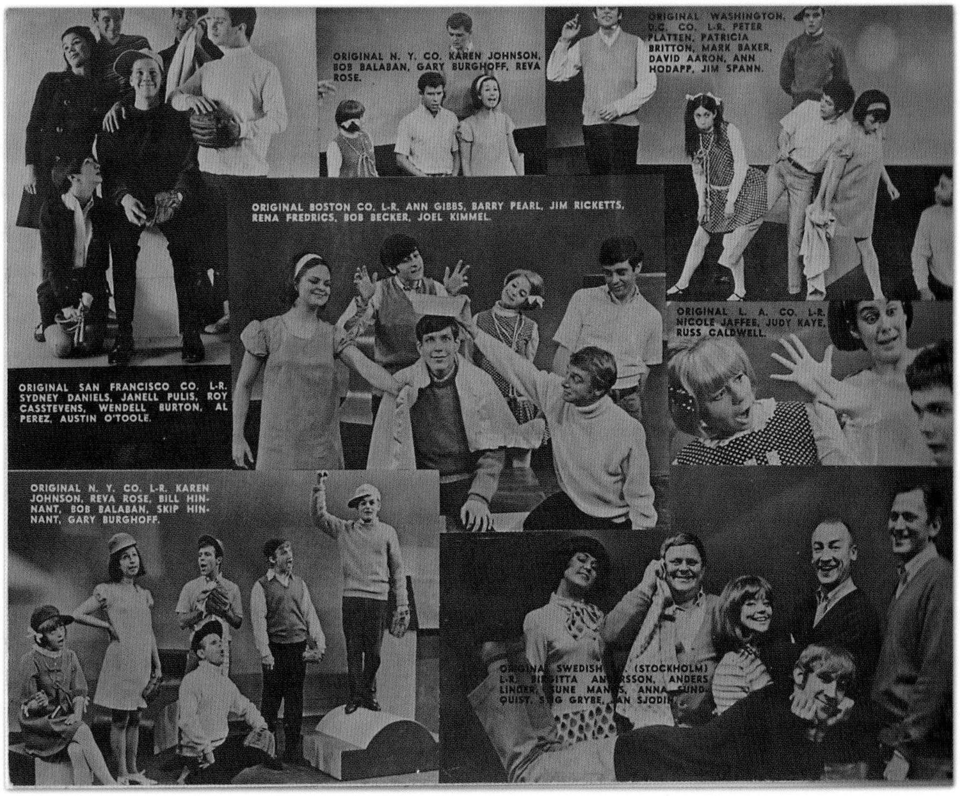

ORIGINAL N. Y. CO. KAREN JOHNSON, BOB BALABAN, GARY BURGHOFF, REVA ROSE.
ORIGINAL WASHINGTON, D.C. CO. L-R. PETER PLATTEN, PATRICIA BRITTON, MARK BAKER, DAVID AARON, ANN HODAPP, JIM SPANN.
ORIGINAL BOSTON CO. L-R. ANN GIBBS, BARRY PEARL, JIM RICKETTS, RENA FREDRICS, BOB BECKER, JOEL KIMMEL.
ORIGINAL L. A. CO. L-R. NICOLE JAFFEE, JUDY KAYE, RUSS CALDWELL.
ORIGINAL SAN FRANCISCO CO. L-R. SYDNEY DANIELS, JANELL PULIS, ROY CASSTEVENS, WENDELL BURTON, AL PEREZ, AUSTIN O'TOOLE.
ORIGINAL N. Y. CO. L-R. KAREN JOHNSON, REVA ROSE, BILL HINNANT, BOB BALABAN, SKIP HINNANT, GARY BURGHOFF.

OPPOSITE PAGE: (bottom left) The cast of *Snoopy The Musical* at the Duchess Theatre in London; (bottom center) Arthur Siegel and Kay Ballard, posing with Schulz, known for their 1962 album *Good Grief Charlie Brown! Peanuts*, which predated Broadway's *You're a Good Man, Charlie Brown*; (bottom right) Schulz with *Snoopy's Musical on Ice* performers, including Peggy Fleming in Charlie Brown's garb. **THIS PAGE:** (top right) Theater programs and announcements; (bottom left) cast photos from early productions.

Peanuts in Space

Charlie Brown has been in space . . . once. But boy, did he get there quickly!

In 1969, NASA was preparing to launch Apollo 10, the fourth of its manned space missions, which would involve orbiting the moon and laying the groundwork for Apollo 11 (that flight would place the first people on the moon two months later). Apollo 10's lunar module was to separate from the command module and perform designated maneuvers before redocking. For the sake of radio communications while the two crafts were separated, each needed a call sign. In the spirit of the day, the command module (piloted by John Young) was dubbed "Charlie Brown," while the lunar module (piloted by Gene Cernan) was called "Snoopy."

Under the control of commander Thomas Stafford, they rocketed through space, reaching speeds of over 24,000 miles per hour, at the time the fastest speed ever recorded by a manned vehicle. While orbiting the moon, Young held up drawings of Charlie Brown and Snoopy to the TV cameras, letting the world know that the Peanuts crew had gone where no cartoon character had gone before.

So Snoopy has been to space as well. But then, Snoopy has been to space thousands of times.

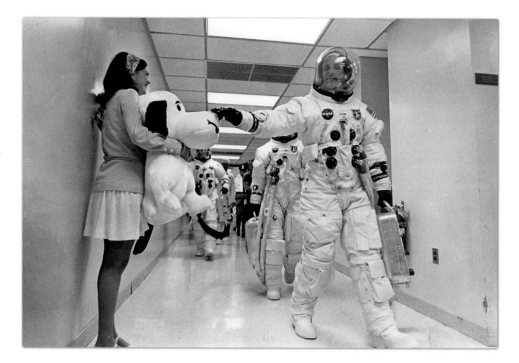

In the 1960s, the space program was big—not just popular and scientifically and politically important, but also physically huge, with countless employees and contractors each working on small pieces of the giant puzzle. To promote quality and attention to detail across the system—in effect, to help get every astronaut home safely—NASA was searching for incentives to offer their workforce. There happened to be a die-hard Snoopy fan heading up the Public Affairs Office at NASA's Manned Spacecraft Center, and he felt that the world's most famous beagle could be key. Al Chop's logic was sound: "Snoopy was a flier; no reason he couldn't become an astronaut, too," he told the *Houston Chronicle* in 2000. Thus was born the Silver Snoopy Award, given to those who have "greatly enhanced space flight safety and mission success."

"It's considered to be the 'astronaut's award.' Just a small percentage of the workforce are able to get this thing," explains NASA's Mike Massimino (the astronaut who brought his toy Snoopy into space). "We are the ones who hand it out. Usually their family is there, and it can be a very touching moment for them. They say it's

the highlight of their career." The award includes a certificate, a letter of commendation, and something extra special: a silver lapel pin with an image of Snoopy in an astronaut suit. "They're all actual flown items," says Massamino, who was accompanied on his space missions in 2002 and 2009 with bags of pins. "Every flight has them."

Anyone wanting to see a Charlie Brown that's been in space can visit the Science Museum in London, where the Apollo 10 spacecraft is on display. To see a Snoopy that's been in space, it's probably easiest to search the lapels of NASA employees, because catching sight of the lunar module Snoopy requires considerably more effort: that Snoopy has spent the last forty-plus years orbiting the sun.

THIS PAGE: (top right) Snoopy gives a warm send-off to the astronauts of the Apollo 10 mission, led here by Astronaut Thomas Stafford, Commander; (bottom) NASA's favorite beagle. OPPOSITE PAGE: (bottom left) A postcard from Bill Melendez to Sparky postmarked October 11, 1968, sent from the Kennedy Space Center; (bottom center) Peanuts patch; (bottom right) the Flying Ace climbs aboard a space shuttle training module.

FEATURED: (above) An animation cel from "The NASA Space Program," an episode in the miniseries *This is America, Charlie Brown*, first aired in 1988. (enclosed) Two Apollo-themed decals, created ca 1969.

2,956
-743
⎯⎯⎯

(55

17

FEATURED: Peppermint Patty in toy, sketch, Christmas ornament, and strip form, displaying three recognizable moods: satisfied, startled, and . . . stumped.

PEANUTS

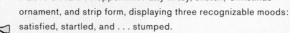

SCHOOL STARTS IN THREE WEEKS, MARCIE, BUT I'M READY...

HOW DOES THIS SOUND TO YOU?

I'VE SIGNED UP FOR BONEHEAD ENGLISH, BONEHEAD MATH, BONEHEAD HISTORY AND BONEHEAD ART...

THAT'S A SCHEDULE I CAN LIVE WITH!

Peppermint Patty

Patricia Reichardt is her name, but she is rarely called that. It's never just "Patty," either, but "Peppermint Patty," or perhaps simply "Sir." Named after the candy, Peppermint Patty burst into the strip in August 1966 as a friend-of-a-friend-of-a-friend from across town who nonetheless managed to insert herself into Charlie Brown's world by briefly taking over as manager of his baseball team (before recognizing the futility of the effort).

From the very start, Peppermint Patty was an enthusiastic tomboy, a mite disheveled but confident in her ability at sports. As time went on, it became clear that she had something more than just quirks akin to what the other characters dealt with (like her inability to recognize that Snoopy was a dog and not a "funny-looking kid with a big nose"). She had academic failings that weren't simply cute malapropisms like Sally's, but an ongoing string of just-above-failing grades. The bad grades may well have been caused by her habit of sleeping in class (certainly, it didn't help), which was in turn due to her staying up at night waiting for her late-working single father, a doting man, to return home. We don't know what happened to Peppermint Patty's mother, just that she's not around. (Peppermint Patty describes herself as having "no mother" with some bitterness.)

Schulz originally intended Peppermint Patty not to be part of the Peanuts cast, but to star in a new strip of her own. Still, adding her to *Peanuts* served the strip well. Her tomboyish nature made her a prime opponent for Charlie Brown on the baseball field and the gridiron, although the teams she headed up generally found little competition on their way to victory.

Peppermint Patty really caught her stride in the 1970s. With Marcie acting as her constant sidekick and sounding board, the strip could focus on her own lack of confidence in academics, romance, and every realm but sport, rather than focusing on the other characters' reaction to her.

The animated world opened up to Peppermint Patty starting with 1967's *You're in Love, Charlie Brown*, voiced by Gail deFaria. Two years later, Gail passed the role over to a sibling for

It Was a Short Summer, Charlie Brown, despite that sibling being her brother Chris. Chris seems untroubled by this, explaining to the documentarians of *Together Again: A Peanuts Voice Cast Reunion* at Comic-Con International in 2008, "For a kid actor to be one of those voices, nothing could be cooler."

The unisex tradition continued, as the list of performers voicing Patty grew to include a Donna, a Linda, a Victoria, and, yes, a Patricia, as well as a Stuart, a Brent, and a Jason. With all those males involved, it almost makes sense that Marcie calls her "sir." Almost.

THIS PAGE: (top left) A 1977 Christmas ornament; (top right) animation cel from *He's Your Dog, Charlie Brown!*; (bottom left) cover of the Hebrew edition of the book *Me, Stressed Out?*; (bottom right): Peppermint Patty holds the playbook in a 1981 drawing created for Aviva Enterprises, Inc., a San Francisco manufacturer.

Sports

Of all the sports to appear in Peanuts, the most memorable has to be baseball, because it was played so constantly and so badly. The strip regularly touched on football as well, or at least the failed place kick attempts (a favorite of many, including Ronald Reagan). But the range of activities tackled is much broader than that: the characters rode surfboards and skateboards, skied and swam, and competed in tennis, motocross, figure skating, bowling, golf, boxing, and roller derby, among other things.

Peanuts always had a strong and visible place for females playing sports, and this became more overt once Schulz met tennis great Billie Jean King. As Jean Schulz notes, "Sparky met Billie Jean in the seventies when we were playing a lot of tennis. He asked her questions about how she kept herself mentally tough on the court. She asked him to illustrate a youth tennis book. It was logical that Billie Jean would talk to him about the Women's Sports Foundation [a nonprofit educational organization which King founded] and that Sparky would agree to help the organization as a board member." He took to using the strip to highlight sportswomen and their issues. Sometimes, the statement was political, like when Marcie said, "in 1978, the average budget for intercollegiate athletics for men was $717,000, but for women it was only $141,000." Sometimes, it was supportive and fanlike; many a female athlete was name-checked. King once wrote that putting her name in a strip was "his way of letting me know that we needed to talk or just catch up with one another."

As big a role as sports had in the strip, they became a practical necessity when it was transferred to animation. Sports allowed for action and visual gags, notably in *You're a Good Sport, Charlie Brown*, the raft race at the center of *Race for Your Life, Charlie Brown*, and even a Charlie Brown appearance at the Super Bowl in a punt-and-pass competition.

Out in the real world, the biggest Peanuts presence is not in baseball, but in golf. The United States Golf Association and the National Golf Foundation both rely on publications featuring Peanuts characters to teach the basics. Then there was the Woodstock Open, an annual golf event held in Santa Rosa, California, that teamed male and female players. "Sparky had always wanted to have the 'mixed doubles' equivalent in golf," explains his wife. "The opportunity came when the Hospice organization asked him to sponsor a golf tournament." Schulz took a great interest in the mechanics of the tournament, which ran for a decade.

Santa Rosa continues to play host to Snoopy's Senior World Hockey Tournament, which has run almost every summer since 1975 at the Redwood Empire Ice Arena, a rink funded by the Schulz family. Teams of players aged forty and older compete round-robin style, with competitions topping out at the seventy-plus age bracket. The lineup has included a number of retired pros, and Schulz himself played until his final tournament in 1999 at age seventy-six.

The Peanuts characters are no strangers to motor sports, either, having adorned cars of such top drivers as Tony Stewart and Bill Elliott. On August 5, 2000, NASCAR champion Jeff Gordon ran a car featuring images of Woodstock and Snoopy. Charlie Brown might have been a more appropriate icon for the day—Gordon, who had won the race twice before and would win it twice more in future years, finished in thirty-third place. (Aaugh!)

THIS PAGE: (top left) Woodstock hits the links; (top right) baseball proved fraught with perils from the beginning; (center) Snoopy Collectible Doll, ca 1982. **OPPOSITE PAGE:** Examples of the athleticism inherent to Peanuts, including (top left) Billie Jean King's book and (bottom left) official programs Schulz illustrated for the Sebastopol, California, Little League.

ENCLOSED: Schulz's tongue-in-cheek response letter to a fan eager to give Charlotte Braun the axe.

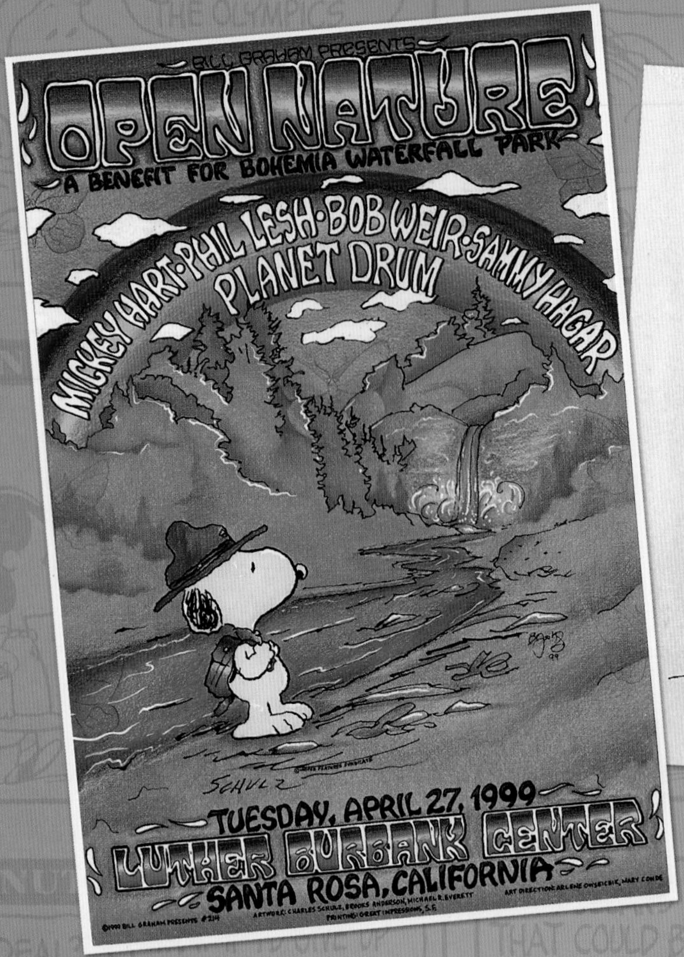
BILL GRAHAM PRESENTS
OPEN NATURE
A BENEFIT FOR BOHEMIA WATERFALL PARK
MICKEY HART·PHIL LESH·BOB WEIR·SAMMY HAGAR
PLANET DRUM
SCHULZ
TUESDAY, APRIL 27, 1999
LUTHER BURBANK CENTER
SANTA ROSA, CALIFORNIA

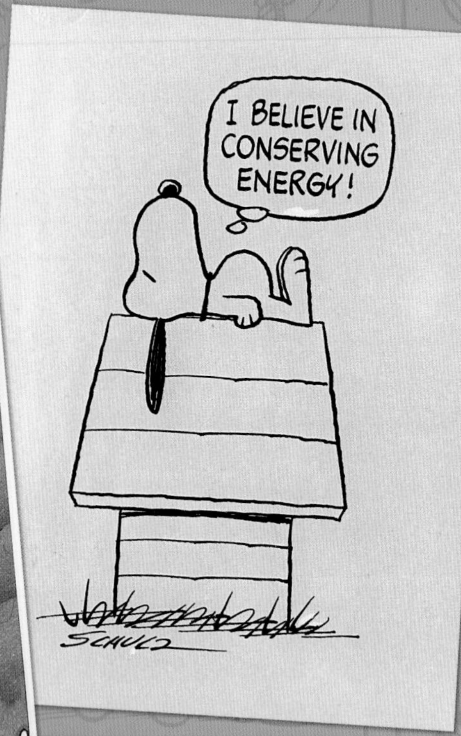
I BELIEVE IN CONSERVING ENERGY!
SCHULZ

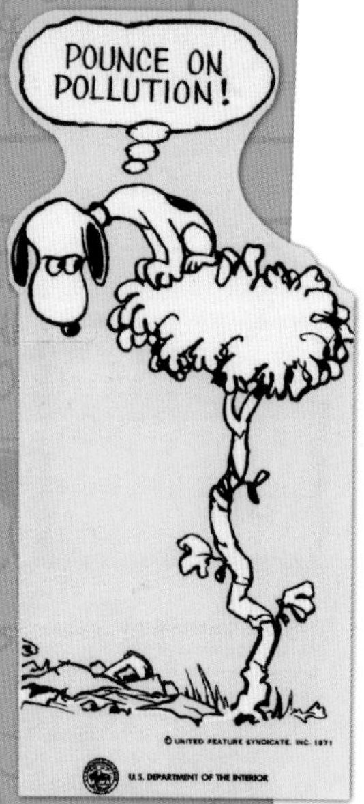
POUNCE ON POLLUTION!
U.S. DEPARTMENT OF THE INTERIOR

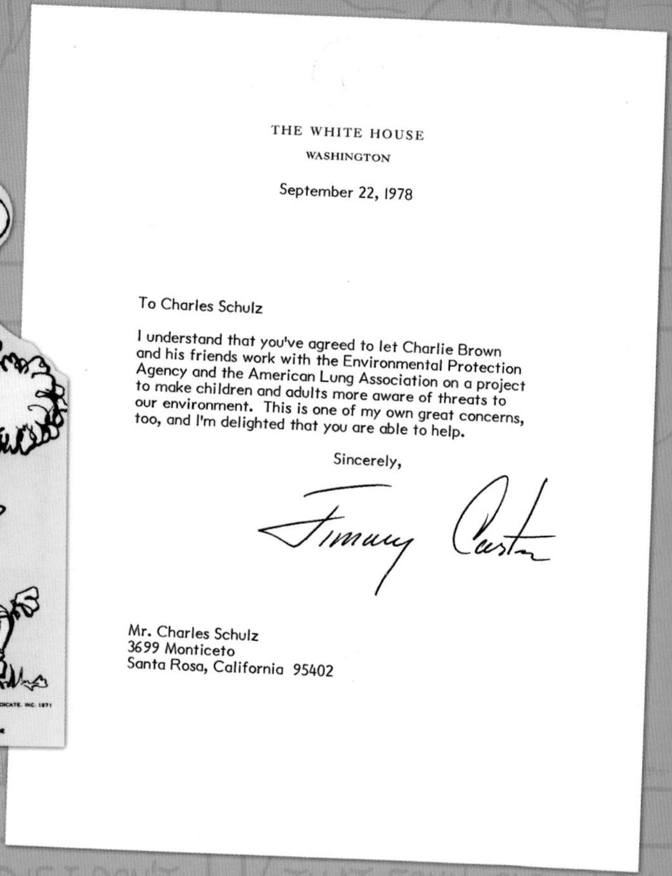

THE WHITE HOUSE
WASHINGTON

September 22, 1978

To Charles Schulz

I understand that you've agreed to let Charlie Brown and his friends work with the Environmental Protection Agency and the American Lung Association on a project to make children and adults more aware of threats to our environment. This is one of my own great concerns, too, and I'm delighted that you are able to help.

Sincerely,

Jimmy Carter

Mr. Charles Schulz
3699 Monticeto
Santa Rosa, California 95402

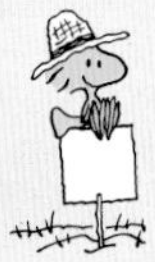

FEATURED: A veritable rainbow of philanthropy, and a letter of thanks from President Jimmy Carter.

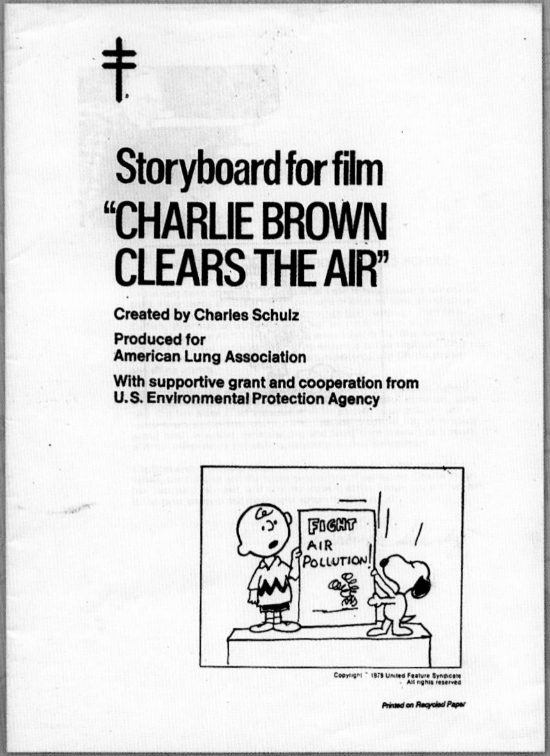

Storyboard for film
"CHARLIE BROWN CLEARS THE AIR"

Created by Charles Schulz

Produced for
American Lung Association

With supportive grant and cooperation from
U.S. Environmental Protection Agency

FIGHT AIR POLLUTION!

Printed on Recycled Paper

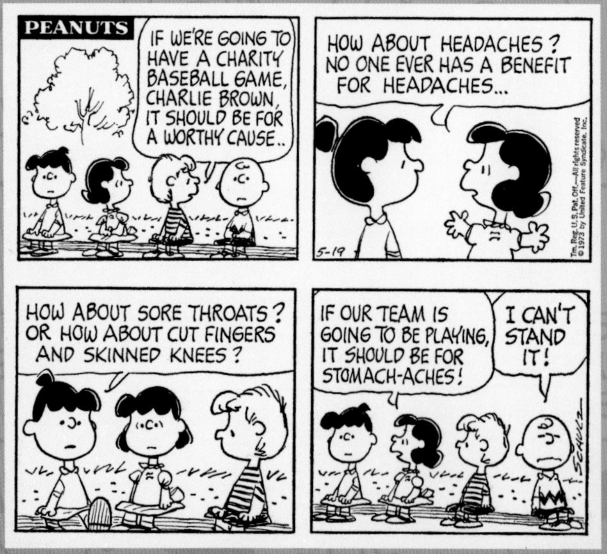
PEANUTS
IF WE'RE GOING TO HAVE A CHARITY BASEBALL GAME, CHARLIE BROWN, IT SHOULD BE FOR A WORTHY CAUSE..
HOW ABOUT HEADACHES? NO ONE EVER HAS A BENEFIT FOR HEADACHES...
HOW ABOUT SORE THROATS? OR HOW ABOUT CUT FINGERS AND SKINNED KNEES?
IF OUR TEAM IS GOING TO BE PLAYING, IT SHOULD BE FOR STOMACH-ACHES!
I CAN'T STAND IT!
SCHULZ

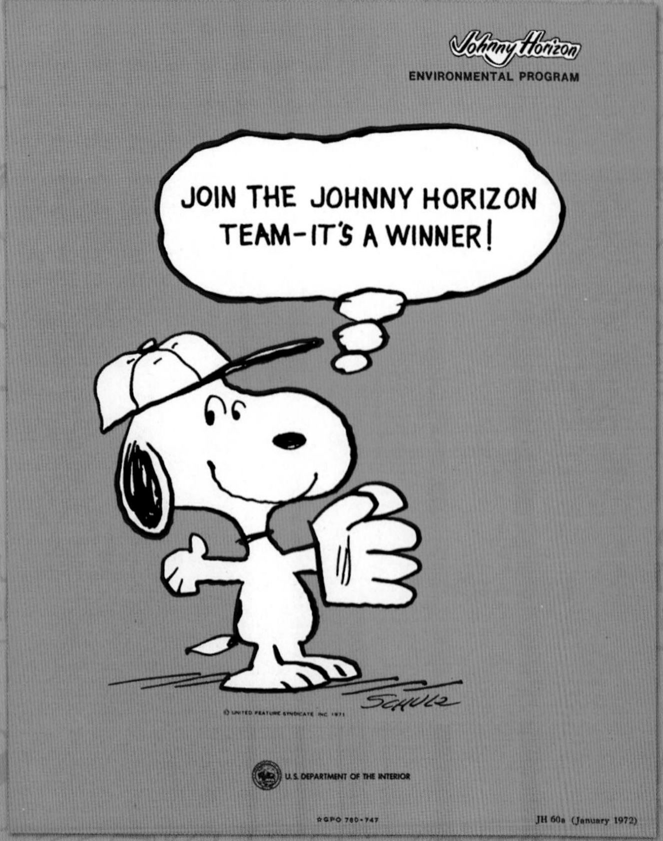
Johnny Horizon
ENVIRONMENTAL PROGRAM
JOIN THE JOHNNY HORIZON TEAM–IT'S A WINNER!
SCHULZ
U.S. DEPARTMENT OF THE INTERIOR
JH 60a (January 1972)

Good Causes

The *Peanuts* strip was always first and foremost a piece of entertainment, but that didn't keep Schulz from using it to educate and inspire. Most often he took on topics related to children's health. For example, in late 1965, Charlie Brown gave his sister Sally an eye test, and she was diagnosed with amblyopia—more commonly known as "lazy eye." Traditional treatment calls for the patient to cover up the properly functioning eye for extended periods, forcing the impacted eye to compensate. And so for a full six months, readers opened their morning paper to see Sally wearing an eye patch, a constant reminder that amblyopia exists and is treatable.

In 1967, the U.S. government launched a campaign to eradicate measles. *Peanuts* spent the first week of the year on Linus and Lucy's trip to the doctor's office for their measles vaccination. The strip maintained its sense of humor—a child's dread at facing the needle can be hilarious to everyone but the child in question—but it also conveyed the danger of measles and the value of the shot. Ultimately, Linus is won over and triumphant, and (as Linus is wont to do) turns into a proselytizer. These strips were reprinted in giveaway booklets to help spread the word.

Spreading the word on important subjects was not limited to the strip. The Peanuts animation team partnered with the American Dental Association to create short films teaching kids how to brush ("Toothbrushing with Charlie Brown") and floss ("It's Dental Flossophy, Charlie Brown"). In 1978, a three-way collaboration between the Peanuts animation group, the American Lung Association, and the United States Environmental Protection Agency put together the short film "Charlie Brown Clears the Air." In the midst of the usual Peanuts antics and baseball games, the viewer is treated to messages about the environmental impact of burning leaves, poorly maintained heaters, and dogs driving motorbikes that are in need of a tune-up.

When the American Cancer Society reached out for a short film about children with cancer, the Peanuts folks instead delivered a full-length animated special and a published book, both titled *Why, Charlie Brown, Why?* The story focuses on the Peanuts gang reacting to a new character, Janice, undergoing an ultimately successful course of chemotherapy.

When it comes to charity causes, the most frequently used member of the cast is a certain spokesbeagle. Naturally, Snoopy is popular in campaigns about dogs. Some of those campaigns are for the dogs' benefit, such as the bumper stickers using Snoopy to advertise the dangers of pups riding in the beds of pickup trucks. Other times, it's to help dogs serve people: When Canine Companions for Independence, a group that provides trained assistance dogs for the disabled, needed help, they called on Snoopy. It was his letter (written with the help of Schulz's widow, Jean) to Trouble Helmsley—famed canine heir of hotelier Leona Helmsley—that helped secure the group a $100,000 grant from the Leona M. and Harry B. Helmsley Charitable Trust.

THIS PAGE: (attached) Sally and Charlie Brown in an educational booklet explaining amblyopia, ca 1968; (top right) Woodstock joins the fight against pollution; (bottom right) the whole gang gets into the act.

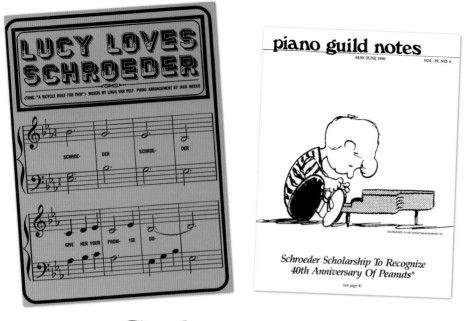

Schroeder

Beethoven is Beethoven; Brahms is Brahms; Mozart is Mozart. They need no other names to be identified. Similarly, Schroeder is Schroeder; he is never given a first name. Or perhaps he's never given a *last* name—even that is never made explicit, although Schulz did take the name "Schroeder" from a coworker at St. Paul's Highland Park Golf Course, where he worked as a caddy in his teenage years.

Schroeder is focused. He's a musician—and not just a musician, but a *classical* musician, somehow eking sweet longhair music out of a toy piano where "the black keys," as Charlie Brown points out, "are just painted on." He is generally well versed in classical music, but his obsession is Ludwig van Beethoven. He plays a lot of Beethoven, he has a cupboard filled with Beethoven statues, he collects Beethoven trading cards, and he turns Beethoven's birthday into a holiday—despite the fact that, as the American Beethoven Society notes in its online exhibition *Schulz's Beethoven: Schroeder's Muse*, "ironically, we don't know the exact date of Beethoven's birth." "The name Beethoven," Schulz would explain, "is funnier than Brahms."

But Schroeder isn't a monomaniac; he does have a life when he's not behind the keyboard. In the winter he plays hockey, and in the spring and summer he's the catcher on Charlie Brown's baseball team, a position that gives him both a good view of bad pitching and a mask that at least partially protects him from unwanted amorous attention. He displays no interest in romance, which makes him the perfect comedic foil for the attentions of Lucy.

Schulz took great care in his depiction of Schroeder, and particularly of Schroeder's music. Not content with the usual cartoon practice of throwing a few stray music notes onto the page to indicate the presence of music, Schulz copied the entire score. He delved into Beethoven's history to find bits that would serve as the basis for a strip. When Schroeder screams at Lucy that "You never cared that the countess turned him down, or that Therese married the baron instead of him or that Lobkowitz stopped his annuity!!", you knew that Schulz had done his homework. He later admitted that he'd been saving that one up. "For a long time," he wrote in *Peanuts Jubilee*, the strip's twenty-fifth anniversary book, "I had thought that the sentence 'Lobkowitz had stopped his annuity' was an extremely funny sentence, and I was happy to find a way to use it."

Schulz had that eye for comedy. It's unlikely that anyone else who had read that sentence before had seen its potential. It was certainly a serious situation for Beethoven, and a dour matter for Schroeder, but put that unlikely phrase into the mouth of a boy filled with obsessive passion, and it's a gem indeed.

THIS PAGE: (top) Sheet music and announcement of a Schroeder Scholarship launched in 1990. OPPOSITE PAGE: (top left) Title panel for a Sunday strip; (top right) a hand-carved wooden music box crafted in Italy in 1968; (bottom) Lucy strikes out again.

 FEATURED: (center right) Cocktail napkin from a box of thirty-six featuring various four-paneled strips, ca 1970.

I ALWAYS THOUGHT BEETHOVEN WAS A NATIVE OF MINNESOTA!

SCHROEDER

ENCLOSURE: (in pocket) Harriet Glickman's 1968 letter to Schulz, encouraging integration in the strip.

I GOT SIX COMPLIMENTS TODAY... AND TWO OF THEM WERE EVEN SINCERE!

SNOOPY only lands on Toxic-Free Lawns!

PEANUTS
© UNITED FEATURE SYNDICATE, INC.

Make sure YOUR yard is Chemical Pesticide-Free for the safety of yourself, your children and your pets!

A MESSAGE FOR PARENTS AND PET OWNERS

A Fawcett Crest Book   THIS IS A DIFFERENT KIND OF PEANUTS BOOK.

What's It All About, Charlie Brown?

MY BOOKS! MY RECORDS! MY POOL TABLE! MY VAN GOGH!
GOOD GRIEF!
SOB!

by JEFFREY H. LORIA

When Do The Good Things Start?

PSYCHIATRIC HELP 5¢
THE DOCTOR IS IN

A therapist looks at life's ups and downs (with a bit of help from Charlie Brown and his friends)

ABRAHAM J. TWERSKI, M.D.

PEANUTS
LOOK, CHARLIE BROWN... I GOT A NEW BASEBALL BAT FOR MY BIRTHDAY!
I CAN HARDLY WAIT FOR NEXT SEASON TO TRY IT OUT!
WHO'S NAME IS ON IT... MICKEY MANTLE? WILLIE MAYS?
IT MUST BE A GIRL'S BAT...
IT SAYS, "RACHEL CARSON"
11-12

PEANUTS
IS YOUR WHOLE FAMILY HERE AT THE BEACH, FRANKLIN?
NO, MY DAD IS OVER IN VIETNAM
MY DAD'S A BARBER.. HE WAS IN A WAR, TOO, BUT I DON'T KNOW WHICH ONE
DO YOU LIKE BASEBALL, CHARLIE BROWN?
MY PROBLEM IS I LIKE BASEBALL TOO MUCH
ARE YOU A GOOD PLAYER?
I HAVE SOME FRIENDS WHO WOULD REGARD THAT AS A GREAT TOPIC FOR A PANEL DISCUSSION

Breaking New Ground

Peanuts is known as a smart strip, as an insightful strip, but also as a safe strip. It's not seen as a *Doonesbury*, whose in-your-face politics are expected to offend some part of its audience, nor is it seen like Morrie Turner's *Wee Pals*, where a multicultural cast serves to provide important but sometimes heavy-handed lessons. But perhaps it's this very impression of *Peanuts* as sweet and safe that allowed it to carry its message so effectively at times.

In September 1962, natural historian Rachel Carson published her groundbreaking and controversial book *Silent Spring*, bringing attention to the effects of pesticides and providing a key spark to the environmental movement. Just two months later, *Peanuts* started depicting her as a hero . . . not by arguing her point, but by having Lucy mention that her baseball bat is signed not by Mickie Mantle or Willie Mays, but by Rachel Carson. The strip soon showed Carson as someone worth quoting (Lucy does so) and emulating (Linus criticizes Lucy for not doing so). In ways, the Peanuts crew is still standing up for her decades later. Snoopy acts as spokesdog for the Rachel Carson Council's campaign against chemical lawn pesticides, which have a strong impact on pets (even a World War I Flying Ace has to land sometime).

In the 1960s, the strip ruffled some feathers when it integrated the comics page by introducing Franklin. Now Franklin may seem an inoffensive soul (indeed, he lacks the quirks that mark most of the Peanuts cast), but at the time integration of the public schools was still meeting strong resistance in parts of the United States. In April 1968, schoolteacher Harriet Glickman wrote Schulz a letter, encouraging him to integrate the strip's cast. Schulz wrote back, confessing that he was "faced with the same problem that other cartoonists are," explaining the widely felt concern that introducing African-American characters would seem patronizing.

"And I said, well why don't I run this idea past two or three of my African-American friends?" Glickman recalls, "and I did, and one of them sent a letter, and before that letter came he wrote back and said 'I'm doing it.'" Seeing African-American Franklin playing with Caucasian Charlie Brown, or in class alongside white students in the school district he attended with Peppermint Patty, discomforted some readers, and the move received coverage in *Newsweek* and elsewhere. Glickman is proud of the results of her encouragement: "I always refer to Franklin as my fourth child."

Religion, also a touchy subject on the comics page, was rarely addressed. Yet *Peanuts* discussed religion on a number of levels, some purely allegorical—like the question of blind faith in The Great Pumpkin year after year—and some simply an acknowledgment that religion existed—like the Peanuts kids talking theology on the baseball field. Linus demonstrated strong knowledge of

the Bible; his topping off *A Charlie Brown Christmas* with a recitation from the Gospel of Luke truly stood out, reminding viewers of the holiday's meaning. But the strip didn't shy away from critical comments on religious belief, either. Surely, Snoopy had some reason when in 1976 he wrote a book on theology entitled *Has It Ever Occurred to You That You Might Be Wrong?*—a phrase Linus later invokes in a discussion at a harsh, religious-oriented camp. That storyline had Peppermint Patty terrified by the camp's we're-in-the-last-days theology . . . a fear that turned to scorn when she learned that the camp was simultaneously raising funds to build a new camp. "Maybe the world will end tomorrow," she notes, "but I wasn't born yesterday."

OPPOSITE PAGE: (top left) A Franklin keychain with moveable arms and head, ca 2004; (bottom left) speculation on the philosophy of *Peanuts* is well-worn publishing territory; (bottom right) subtly groundbreaking strips. **THIS PAGE:** (top right) Franklin and Linus in an original drawing created for the book *Things I've Had to Learn Over and Over and Over*, ca 1986.

Unrequited Love

Love, specifically romantic love, drives so much of Peanuts. That would make the characters' lives wonderful, if it wasn't for one problematic fact: almost all of the love is unrequited.

Consider Sally Brown, who carries in her heart a demanding love for Linus. She courts him in her way, sending valentines addressed to "My Sweet Babboo," a term he recognizes as being addressed at him, but fails to accept. "I used to call Sparky 'my sweet babboo,' and then one day it was in the comic strip," explains Schulz's widow, Jeannie. "I think it came from another expression—I used to call him 'poor sweet baby,' which also appeared in the strip. So from poor sweet baby to sweet babboo is not such a big leap."

Linus has his own romantic entanglements. One of these is a straightforward kid crush on his teacher, Miss Othmar, and in some ways it's the least damaging of all crushes in the strip. He doesn't seem to seek reciprocation; he's content with being "very fond of the ground on which she walks." More troublesome is the girl who sits behind him in class, a befuddling soul who asks to be called different names (most commonly, "Lydia"), gives him a fake address, and constantly spurns advances he hasn't actually made yet. "Aren't you too old for me?" she asks the young lad two months her senior. It's not clear whether Linus has any real interest in her, but her playing hard-to-get clearly drives him to frustration, and where there is frustration, there may be love.

And where there is love, there may be frustration, as Linus's big sister can attest. The often-harsh Lucy can be quite gentle as she leans against Schroeder's piano, spinning descriptions of the married life she plans to share with that young musician. Her plans, alas, have one fatal flaw: Schroeder himself, who is quick to yank the figurative rug (not to mention the literal piano) out from under her dreams.

But if there's a king of unrequited love, it's Charlie Brown, whose affection for the Little Red-Haired Girl burns intensely within him. This trait was inspired in ways by someone in Schulz's own life, Donna Johnson, whom he called "little red-haired

girl." Schulz once asked Johnson, a coworker at Art Instruction School, to marry him—and was turned down. Yet Charlie Brown's Little Red-Haired Girl situation is more tragic, in that she does not spurn him in any way, because she's never given the chance: he is too fearful and too certain of rejection to even approach her.

But Charlie Brown shouldn't be so convinced he's unlovable—not only do millions of readers adore him; characters in the strip do as well. It took Peppermint Patty years to accept that she wanted affection from a kid she could "strike out on three straight pitches," but ultimately she found herself competing with her sidekick Marcie for "Chuck's" affections—a competition that Charlie Brown seems utterly unaware of.

The happy news is that Charlie Brown's affection does eventually get requited, by a girl at summer camp in 1990. He calls her "Peggy Jean"; she calls him "Brownie Charles." (He was flustered when he introduced himself.) Even though she eventually finds another boyfriend, until then he is able to talk to her and to share some childhood romance. On the scale of Charlie Brown's accomplishments, that's a triumph indeed.

It's amazing how stupid you can be when you're in love...

NOTHING IS MORE EMPTY THAN AN EMPTY MAILBOX..

IF YOU PUT YOUR EAR UP REAL CLOSE, YOU CAN HEAR THE OCEAN ROAR..

© 1993 United Feature Syndicate, Inc.

10-19

THIS PAGE: (top right) Schulz drew this for Donna Johnson, who was very likely his inspiration for the strip's Little Red-Haired Girl; (center) Lucy says it all. **OPPOSITE PAGE:** (center left) Schroeder eternally captivates—and frustrates—Lucy; (bottom left) two images distributed by CBS to promote *It's Your First Kiss, Charlie Brown* (1977) and *Be My Valentine, Charlie Brown* (1975); (bottom right) a sweet sentiment.

ENCLOSURE: A kind letter from Charlie Brown to a fan. (on pouch) The letter's envelope.

C/O M Sgt. R. F. Hobson

Co "A" S&MA (SED)

APO New York, New York 09058

I look forward to the day when I'll understand men.

MAYBE YOU SHOULD GIVE UP THIS INSANE LOVE AFFAIR.. JUST LET THINGS HAPPEN ..THAT'S WHAT I'VE DONE WITH MY SWEET BABBOO...

I'M NOT YOUR SWEET BABBOO!

8-4

© 1984 United Feature Syndicate, Inc.

Copr. © 1977 United Feature Syndicate, Inc.

VALENTINES FOR THOSE WE LOVE

Love is walking hand in hand.

51

- PROCLAMATION -

HONORING "SPIKE" AND PROCLAIMING JULY 4, 1981, AS "SPIKE DAY" IN THE CITY OF NEEDLES, CALIFORNIA

WHEREAS, Charles M. Schulz has given much publicity to the City of Needles through his Peanuts cartoon character known as "Spike"; and

WHEREAS, Spike has made many excursions to the City of Needles in his adventurous travels; and

WHEREAS, Spike always has been and always will be a welcomed resident of the City of Needles; and

WHEREAS, Spike has now entered into business within the City, known as "Spike Realtor Associate", selling choice properties in the area; and

WHEREAS, we, the people of the City of Needles, do sincerely wish Spike the best of luck in his endeavors.

NOW, THEREFORE, I, DAVID B. DANIEL, Mayor of the City of Needles, California, by the authority vested in me, do hereby issue this proclamation in honor of "Spike"; and further, do hereby declared July 4, 1981, as

"SPIKE DAY"

within the City of Needles, and urge all citizens to join in honoring Spike on this day.

DAVID B. DANIEL, MAYOR
CITY OF NEEDLES, CALIFORNIA

FEATURED: Certificate from the Mayor of Needles, California, proclaiming official "Spike Day" in 1981.

WE NEED MORE PAPER...

I WENT INTO NEEDLES YESTERDAY, AND TALKED TO A PSYCHIATRIST...

I ASKED HIM IF TALKING TO A CACTUS WAS A SIGN I WAS GOING CRAZY...

"NO," HE SAID, "ONLY IF THE CACTUS STARTS TO TALK BACK!"

PLEASE DON'T SAY ANYTHING...

© 1985 United Feature Syndicate, Inc.

Spike & Company

Snoopy was born on the Daisy Hill Puppy Farm, and like most puppies, he did not come into this world alone. In fact, he's one of a litter of eight, although we never get to meet the entire crew. Making his debut in 1975, long-whiskered Spike was the first of the siblings to pop up and truly be a major player in the second half of the strip's run. He manages to avoid landing in a traditional home, instead somehow thriving in the desert of Needles, California. And though he pays Snoopy a visit from time to time—and at one point succumbs to the temptations of human-assisted living, visibly packing weight onto his skinny frame—he is seen most often on his own turf, amusing himself in the company of sagebrush and cacti.

In many ways, Spike's desert strips were very different from the main Peanuts strips, almost entirely devoid of interaction with or inspiration from other characters. Spike's are strange narratives about a lonely soul compelled to anthropomorphize the plants around him because they're the only company he has. At most, he is interacting by correspondence, and even then the reality is in doubt—is Mickey Mouse truly sending him gifts, or has the desert heat merely gotten to our protagonist? The Spike strips are at times abstract or even downright weird, and often reminiscent of an improv show performed by a single man on stage with limited props.

Needles is a real town. Not only that, it's a real *hot* town; temperatures there have gotten as high as 125 degrees Fahrenheit, and on some days the thermometer never dips below 90. Schulz knew this place well, since his family had moved there when he was six, staying for a couple years before returning to the cooler climate of Minnesota. At the time, it was a town of around 3,000, and it's not that much bigger now. He knew it would make a great locale for an isolated character who may have been driven a bit mad by the heat. Schulz added an even more personal touch, as "Spike" was the name of his boyhood dog.

Spike got his own TV showcase in *It's the Girl in the Red Truck, Charlie Brown*. This uniquely hour-long, animation/live-action hybrid only briefly features Charlie Brown and Snoopy, and none of the other usual Peanuts gang. The main star besides Spike is that Peanuts rarity, an adult—and a real one at that. The special was cowritten by Schulz's son Monte, and the title "Girl" is played by Schulz's daughter Jill.

Snoopy and Spike's family also includes a sister, Belle, and three brothers, Olaf, Marbles, and Andy, all of whom appear infrequently (often together). Belle looks a lot like a feminized Snoopy, with long eyelashes and hairbows—well, ear bows. She also has a teenaged son. Rotund brother Olaf once won an "ugly dog" contest and bites "only if attacked by a pizza." Marbles is the speckle-eared, wide-eyed brother who has lived with a number of families and spent time as a research dog. As for Andy, when asked what makes him different, Snoopy writes, "Andy was fuzzy." Indeed he is.

Rounding out the clan are a brother (Rover) and sister (Molly) who appear only in TV specials— and in Schulz's view, facts established in the TV specials don't count.

OPPOSITE PAGE: (top left) Roly-poly Olaf; (top center) sketches of Spike ca 1975; (center left) an unfinished strip that Schulz ripped before throwing away, later retrieved; (bottom right) a plush Andy from 1992.
THIS PAGE: (top right) A rubbery plastic Spike; (bottom right, on and under flap) sketch and finished Spike scene.

IF WE'RE ALL BROTHERS, HOW COME I'M SO FUZZY, YOU'RE SO SKINNY AND OLAF IS SO FAT?

I'M NOT SKINNY.. I'M TRIM!

AND I'M NOT FAT!

YOU'RE NOT FAT?

I'M ROLY-POLY!

SCHULZ

SCHULZ

TOM EVERHART
SNOOPY IN PAINTING

こんなスヌーピー見たことない！

『ピーナッツ』の原作者シュルツ氏が
スヌーピーを描くことを認めた世界で唯一のアーティスト

定価 3980円　本体 3790円　扶桑社

ARCHITECTS FOR SNOOPY

ALL I REALLY WANT IS...

THE MONTREAL MUSEUM OF FINE ARTS

CHARLES M. SCHULZ
AT THE LOUVRE

Speak Softly and Carry a Beagle: The Art of Charles Schulz

Snoopy

Charles Schulz, 1994. Photo Credit: Robert Schilling

Charles Schulz, 1990. Photo Credit: Giovanni Trimboli

Woodstock

Charlie Brown

Lucy

Schroeder

Linus

Pig Pen

November 3, 2001 through May 5, 2002
The Norman Rockwell Museum
at Stockbridge

Hallmark

National Tour Sponsor of *Speak Softly and Carry a Beagle: The Art of Charles Schulz*.
Organized by the Minnesota Museum of American Art, Saint Paul, MN and
the Charles M. Schulz Museum, Santa Rosa, CA.

Peppermint Patty

Snoopy

FEATURED: (top left) Catalog cover from
Tom Everhart's 2000 Snoopy exhibit in Japan;
(top right) Poster for Schulz's Louvre debut.

54

Peanuts in the World of Art

While Schulz found decades of respect as a cartoonist, as an entertainer, and as a producer of popular culture, he didn't expect his comic strip to be taken as fine art; comic strips were tossed away with the daily paper, it was the nature of the beast.

It was by happy accident that artist Tom Everhart discovered a different light to cast on Peanuts: while working on an assignment creating posters for MetLife, Everhart placed some of Schulz's artwork in a projector and accidentally magnified it, beaming Schulz's line-work across his walls and creating "these extraordinary, elegant black lines . . . presiding over my dark studio like suspension cables stretching across a bridge that gracefully wiggle from tower to tower," as he later wrote.

Sparked by this, Everhart set out to produce large oil paintings and prints inspired by Schulz's work. The art world embraced them and exhibitions have included "Tom Everhart: Snoopy in Paintings" in 2000 at Japan's Suntory Museum.

Two cities have played host to larger-than-life versions of Schulz's art: Saint Paul, Minnesota, (his boyhood home) and Santa Rosa, California, (home to his office for most of his cartooning career). Each site hosted a series of events—Saint Paul from 2001 to 2004, and Santa Rosa from 2005 to 2007—in which as many as a hundred or more artists were invited each year to decorate a character in his or her own style—some reverent, some whimsical, some commercial. The statues were then placed around the city, inviting tourists to view all the Snoopys, Woodstocks, Lucys, or whichever the year's featured figure. After the exhibition, most of the statues were auctioned for charity.

"The statue program was a huge success on many levels," says Schulz's son Craig, who was on the steering committee for the Santa Rosa events. "We raised many times more money to fund the programs we had set out to fund: a bronze [statue] at the Charles Schulz Airport and a scholarship for aspiring artists. The one word that sums up the whole project is 'smiles.' I have never been witness to an event where each and every day you could just stand and watch grandparents, parents, and children and no one was complaining."

Other artists got to take their stab at Peanuts for a 1992 Montreal Museum of Fine Arts exhibit, "Snoopy the Masterpiece." Fifteen architects were asked to create drawings and models imagining a new doghouse for Snoopy. The results ranged from a single I-beam with a small door slot to Snoopy's very own flying saucer.

But the clearest example of Peanuts finding a place in the art world came years prior when, in 1990, Schulz became the first American cartoonist to have a retrospective at the world's most visited museum, the Louvre in Paris. Pig-Pen and pals were now hanging in the

**Charlie Brown
A Boy For All Seasons:
20 Years
on Television**
AT THE MUSEUM OF BROADCASTING

same institution as some of the most widely acknowledged masterpieces. This was not the first such display—there had been a Peanuts show at the Oakland Museum five years earlier—nor would it be the last, but in the art world there is no institution more prestigious than the Louvre. The *Ordre des Arts et des Lettres* that was bestowed on Schulz by the French Ministry of Culture was just icing on that cake.

OPPOSITE PAGE: (top center) Brochure cover from a special exhibit in Montreal; (center) dressed as a conductor, Charlie Brown touched down in Santa Rosa's Railroad Square during the 2005 Peanuts on Parade event; (bottom left) an exhibition hosted at the Norman Rockwell Museum in Stockbridge, MA, in 2001–02; (bottom right) preparations for a public installation in Kobe, Japan. **THIS PAGE:** (top right) Museum of Broadcasting Catalogue; (bottom center) Snoopy art displayed for the 45th anniversary of Peanuts and the 28th of NASA's relationship with Schulz.

FEATURED: (center right) Sketched versions of Rerun investigating a bag, bordered by Schulz's thoughts on the story line of a November 1998 strip. (bottom right) Linus and Rerun in the woods.

Younger Siblings

Charlie Brown took on a major new role in 1959, announcing to the world, "I'm a father!" He maintained enthusiasm while quickly correcting himself: "I mean my *Dad's* a father! I'm a brother! I have a baby sister!" Thus arrived Sally Brown. Sharing her brother's bowling ball–shaped head (although, thankfully, not his bowling ball–like lack of hair), Sally began her life as a cute little thing for Charlie Brown to push around in a stroller.

She would not let him or anyone else push her around for long. Sally quickly developed major, if often misplaced, confidence. She struggled in school but didn't view herself as failing; rather, the school was failing *her*. The system placed unreasonable demands on her and failed to appreciate her knowledge—that "Abraham Lincoln was our sixteenth king, and the father of Lot's wife," or that "family life among the Egyptians was easier than it is today" because "they were all facing the same way." In the later years she adopted a series of personal philosophies, starting with "Who cares?" or "Why me?" and eventually landing on one that would fuel her education: "I've

decided to put everything off until the last minute and to learn everything in life the hard way."

Rerun Van Pelt was the last major human character to enter the Peanuts canon, and he didn't start out major. When introduced in May of 1972, he wasn't even seen. Linus and Lucy were told they had a new baby brother. Lucy, tired enough of having one brother, declared him a "rerun"; Linus seized the label for the unseen tyke, and the unlikely name stuck. As Linus then observed, "Babies really aren't very interesting. Babies just sleep and cry." Thus, Rerun remained unseen for almost a year. Once sighted, he was clearly a Van Pelt, right down to the Fender Stratocaster

head. He played one game on Charlie Brown's baseball team, then spent decades confined mostly to the back seat of his mother's careening bicycle.

During the 1990s Rerun came into his own, starting school and adopting the role of the outsider. The other kids happily ignored him. Only Snoopy took him seriously, and sometimes had to be bribed with cookies to do so.

Most Peanuts characters can be defined in terms of what they want but *don't* get: Charlie Brown wants to win the ball game, launch his kite, be loved by the Little Red-Haired Girl, and kick the football. Lucy wants the world to bend to her will, and to get the attention of Schroeder. Schroeder wants to be left alone. Rerun's frustrated desires are interestingly normal and reasonable: he just wants a dog and a bicycle. Alas, he must make do with the back of his mother's bike and the occasional borrowed dog.

While he had small roles on TV as far back as 1976's *It's Arbor Day, Charlie Brown*, Rerun didn't get a key on-screen role until the twenty-first century as a major player in the specials *I Want a Dog for Christmas, Charlie Brown* and *He's a Bully, Charlie Brown*.

Late in the strip's run, Schulz passed his own childhood ambition on to Rerun: the youngest Van Pelt wanted to be a cartoonist. Given Rerun's ability to hustle dog-buying funds, it would come as no surprise if he eventually did earn his living in the field of underground comics (or, as he called them, "basement comics"). It was, perhaps, a gift from Schulz to his young character to give him an ambition that was both achievable and rewarding.

OPPOSITE PAGE: (top left) A storyboard for *I Want a Dog for Christmas, Charlie Brown!* (2003); (top right) Rerun and Snoopy; (bottom left) Sally's school book; (center) a large Hungerford doll of Charlie Brown's sister as a baby, ca 1959. **THIS PAGE:** (center left) Rerun's usual seat; (center) plastic Sally, grown up (a little bit).

End of an Era

No human lasts forever, and neither does any human endeavor. On November 16, 1999, Charles Schulz had a stroke. Under hospital care, it was discovered that this wasn't the end of the bad news; he also had aggressive colon cancer. If there was to be any hope of him drawing again, it would only be after a long and slow recovery. On December 14, it was announced to the world that he was retiring, bringing an end to new installments of the daily strip. Publicly, family members were expressing confidence that he would pull through, perhaps continue working on Peanuts stories in a comic book format, which would not have as relentless a deadline as a daily strip. Privately, it was understood that time was likely short.

The final daily appeared on January 3, 2000; it was a typeset goodbye note from Schulz to his readers and his characters. Because Sunday comic strips are prepared farther in advance than weekday strips, new material continued appearing on Sundays into February. In the week leading up to the final Sunday—a rerunning of the farewell note with more art reused from earlier strips—TV networks ran tribute shows saying goodbye to *Peanuts*.

That final Sunday comic was in newspapers that hit readers' driveways on February 13. Sparky had been sent an early copy of a Sunday insert, so he had seen it. He passed away in his sleep on Saturday night, mere hours before a copy of the full Sunday paper would be delivered to him. Few who knew him felt it was mere coincidence that he passed on just as his life's work ended.

When Schulz's retirement had been announced, his colleagues in the newspaper cartooning world had hatched a secret plan to honor this man who had inspired and befriended so many. Their objective was to take over the funny pages for one day, with almost every strip doing some sort of tribute to Sparky and Peanuts. On May 27, 2000, the plan was carried out: over 150 different strips paid tribute, some in minor ways, some with full-on paeans to Schulz and his work.

It was not just cartoonists who recognized his greatness. Two days before he passed away, a bill was introduced in the United States Congress to award him the Congressional Gold Medal, the highest honor that the Congress grants to a civilian. It came up for a vote in the House of Representatives on February 15, passing with the overwhelming vote of 410 in favor, 1 against, and then moving on to a unanimous vote in the Senate the following month. Accepting the medal in June of 2001, Jean Schulz noted that Sparky "would have felt an amazingly strong sense of pride and accomplishment knowing that he had been recognized for his important impact on American society." Schulz's son Monte concurred. "It would have been extraordinarily gratifying to receive an award for something that he did every day and that he loved so much."

People had shown that they appreciated all that Schulz had brought the world. Now what was needed was a lasting tribute site, where people could go to reflect on who he was and what he created . . .

THIS PAGE: (top left) Schulz at his drawing board in 1986; (bottom right) Steve Kelley's sentiments.
OPPOSITE PAGE: (top left) Schulz in his office with plush pals, ca 1985; (top right) Gary Markstein's tribute; (bottom left) poster for a holiday show at the ice rink dear to Schulz; (bottom right) the final Sunday strip.

SNOOPY'S

"WONDERFUL MAGICAL
CHRISTMAS"

"An Ice Show the Entire Family Will Love"

STARRING
SCOTT HAMILTON AND SNOOPY
DECEMBER 19th through 28th

at the

REDWOOD EMPIRE ICE ARENA

PSYCHIATRIC
HELP 5¢

THE DOCTOR
IS OUT

BEETHOVEN

HAPPINESS
WAS 50 YEARS
OF "PEANUTS"

SNOOPY

CHARLES M.
SCHULZ

BY ACT OF CONGRESS 2000

FEATURED: (this and opposite page, center) Front and back of the Congressional Gold Medal, awarded posthumously in 2001.

PEANUTS
by Schulz

NO, I
THINK HE'S
WRITING.

Dear Friends...

Dear Friends,
I have been fortunate to draw Charlie Brown and his friends for almost 50 years. It has been the fulfillment of my childhood ambition.
Unfortunately, I am no longer able to maintain the schedule demanded by a daily comic strip. My family does not wish Peanuts to be continued by anyone else,

therefore I am announcing my retirement.
I have been grateful over the years for the loyalty of our editors and the wonderful support and love expressed to me by fans of the comic strip.
Charlie Brown, Snoopy, Linus, Lucy...how can I ever forget them...

Charles M. Schulz

2-13-00

The Legacy Continues

When visitors enter the Charles M. Schulz Museum and Research Center, they are immediately drawn into Schulz's world. The granite facade and wood trim reflect Schulz's no-nonsense Minnesota roots, while his wit and whimsy are found in the kite-eating tree in the courtyard and the thought balloons that provide lighting in the Museum's Great Hall. At the far end of the main hall is a floor-to-ceiling picture of Lucy preparing to pull the football from the hapless Charlie Brown, which on closer inspection is revealed to be a mosaic of thousands of tiles, each containing a complete Peanuts strip. The Museum itself is much like this—at first look, an interesting place to browse through, but on closer examination revealing itself to also be rich with information for academics, researchers, and fans wanting to learn about Schulz's life and work.

The Museum was not Schulz's idea, but even as he continued to create the art that the Museum was to document, he was actively involved in all the major decisions, including the choice of a location near his studio and ice rink in Santa Rosa, California. "Early on when we spoke about it he said, 'It isn't going to be a Disneyland,'" explains Mrs. Schulz. "He had always said the strip was drawn for adults and we agreed that it was to be aimed at readers . . . Sparky's work was done with paper, pen, and ink. That and a fertile mind are what entranced us." The Museum would become the place to reflect and preserve this creative effort.

Schulz passed away before ground was broken in June of 2000. Two years later, on August 17, 2002, the beautiful Museum opened to visitors. It features Schulz's personal effects, a rotating gallery of original Peanuts strip art, and several new exhibitions each year. Some exhibitions focus on specific Peanuts topics; others meet the Museum's mission to "build an understanding of cartoonists and cartoon art." The building has a number of whimsical features, including a nursery wall painted by Schulz for his daughter Meredith in 1951—removed from its original house, relocated, restored, and now on display. The Great Hall features a wooden relief of Snoopy's evolution through the decades by Japanese sculptor Yoshiteru Otani. The courtyard is adorned with life-sized Peanuts statues and an oversized baseball hat. The Museum is also part research center, where Peanuts ephemera and scholarship are catalogued. A vibrant and active collecting organization, the Museum continues to evolve and grow. It attracts fans of all ages and from all countries with lectures and hands-on educational activities, bringing in working cartoonists to speak and engage with Museum patrons. For those who cannot make the journey to Santa Rosa, the Museum's traveling exhibitions now tour venues across the United States.

One prized feature, however, is permanent: on the upper floor, by the top of the stairs, sits Schulz's office, meticulously relocated. Visitors can see the chair he sat in, the drawing board he worked on, and the books he kept around for inspiration or reference or simply because he once put the book on a shelf and never removed it. His tools are also there, including the Esterbrook pen nibs he used until the end, pulled from a private stash he bought when the manufacturer closed down, decades ago. The tranquil room gives us a personal glimpse of the daily routine through which one man with some paper and ink crafted something that brought joy—and continues to bring joy—to hundreds of millions of people around the world.

THIS PAGE: (top left) The Museum entrance; (top right) a close-up of Schulz's tools; (bottom right) the faithful reproduction of his office. OPPOSITE, FAR RIGHT PAGE (INSIDE FLAP): (top left) Walls from a recent Sunday at the Funnies exhibit; (top right) artist Yoshiteru Otani's impressive tiled mosaic; (bottom left) local children enjoying the displays; (bottom right) a Museum archivist carefully preserves the October 17, 1952 comic strip.

Members Opening
Thursday August 15, 2002
4:00 – 6:00PM

CHARLES M.
SCHULZ
MUSEUM

CHARLES M.
SCHULZ
MUSEUM

Members Opening
Thursday August 15, 2002
4:00 – 6:00PM or
Friday August 16, 10:00 – 11:30AM

© U.F.S

AN OPENING CELEBRATION

FEATURED: (top) Invitation, ticket, and hardhat from the Museum's ground breaking; (bottom, l to r) Steve Oliver (Oliver Construction), Schulz Museum Architect C. David Robinson, Santa Rosa Mayor Janet Condron, Snoopy, Santa Rosa City Manager Ken Blackman, and Schulz Museum Board President Jean Schulz at the official groundbreaking ceremony.

Acknowledgments

The author would like to thank John Burdett, Lee Mendelson, Harriet Glickman, Robin Hall, Mike Massamino, Craig Schulz, and Jean Schulz for allowing him to interview them; Amy Wideman and Chris Campbell of becker&mayer! for their support throughout this process; Paige Braddock, Lorrie Adamson, Kim Towner, and Alexis Fajardo of Charles M. Schulz Creative Associates; Lisa Monhoff and Nina Kollmar Fairles of the Charles M. Schulz Museum and Research Center; Jean Sagendorph, Helene Gordon, Allison Mak, and Brandon Carter of United Media for their input, information, and access to archival materials; and Marcie Lee, Derrick Bang, Scott McGuire, Kristy Mendelson, Dean Mullaney, and Allan Holtz for their reference assistance.

Special Thanks

becker&mayer! would like to thank the following for their dedication and insightful contributions to the project: Lisa Monhoff, Nina Kollmar Fairles, and Karen Johnson with the Charles M. Schulz Museum and Research Center; Jean Schulz, Craig Schulz, and Amy Schulz Johnson; Paige Braddock, Alexis Fajardo, Kim Towner, and Pam Drucker at Charles M. Schulz Creative Associates; Jean Sagendorph and Helene Gordon at United Media; Caren Pilgrim and CollectPeanuts.com; Michael Sand and Zinzi Clemmons with Little, Brown and Company; and our devoted author, Nat Gertler.

About the Author

Nat Gertler has, by any sane estimation, far too many Peanuts books. His simple enjoyment of the strip at an early age has snowballed into a reference library of over 1,000 Peanuts- and Schulz-related books. From there, it was a small (but very time-consuming) step to found AAUGH.com, a website featuring a collectors' guide to Peanuts books, as well as The AAUGH Blog (blog.AAUGH.com), a source for news, reviews, and reflection for the Peanuts book fan.

Peanuts also launched Gertler into the world of comics in general. He has written comic books for dozens of publishers, with both well-known characters like Speed Racer and Fred Flintstone and original characters like The Factor and Licensable Bear™. A two-time Eisner Award nominee, he's the cowriter of *The Complete Idiot's Guide to Creating a Graphic Novel*.

He also founded his own publishing and packaging company, About Comics. This allowed him to publish two books of Schulz's non-Peanuts work: *It's Only a Game* collects the complete run of sports and games cartoons that Schulz created for newspaper syndication, and *Schulz's Youth* showcases hundreds of cartoons about teenagers that appeared in Christian youth magazines in the 1950s and 1960s.

Gertler lives in Southern California with his wife, Lara, his children, Ally and Ben, and about two dozen book adaptations of *A Charlie Brown Christmas*.

Foreword contributor **Amy Schulz Johnson** was born Amy Louise Schulz in Minneapolis, where she lived for two years until the Schulz family moved to Sebastopol, California. An avid horseback rider as a child and active in the Mormon Church since her twenties, Amy also enjoyed a successful career in figure skating. She and her husband, Johnny Johnson, have nine children (five girls and four boys) and are proud grandparents. They live in Utah.

Charles M. Schulz, one of the most successful comic strip creators of all time, personally drew and lettered every *Peanuts* strip from its first publication in October 1950 until the final comic in early 2000.

Image Credits

Page 4: Both photos, courtesy of Amy Schulz Johnson; Group sketch, gift of Jean F. Schulz [JFS]; Page 6: Schulz with dog Spike, gift of JFS; Page 7: Schulz at board, © Frank Ross Photo; Page 8: Wrestling sketch, gift of Jeffery J. Pyros & Robert A. Casterline; Sally contact strips, gift of JFS/Tom Vano; Page 9: Drawing strips, gift of JFS/Tom Vano; L'il Folks strip, gift of JFS; Peanuts Album, courtesy of Anderson-Schulz Collection; Page 10: Schulz drawing, courtesy of Bob Martin; Charlie doll, © UFS/Determined Productions/courtesy of Kansas Museum of History/Boucher and Company; Production cel, © UFS/ Bill Melendez Productions [BMP]/Lee Mendleson Productions [LMP]/gift of Jeffrey J. Pyros and Robert A. Casterline; Page 11: Charlie and Lucy sketch, gift of JFS; Spock letter, courtesy of Dr. Benjamin Spock/ gift of JFS; Page 12: Coloring book, © UFS/Saalfield/gift of JFS; View-Master™, © Fisher-Price®; Video game, courtesy of Creative Associates [CA]; Colorforms, © UFS/Colorforms, Inc./courtesy of Freddi Margolin Collection [FMC]; Sally playset, © UFS/Playing Mantis/gift of CA; Page 13: Snoopy figure, © Hungerford Plastics Corp./courtesy of FMC; Linus and Lucy figures, © UFS/Hungerford Plastics Corp; Board game, © UFS/Milton Bradley, Co./courtesy of FMC; Snoopy and Peanuts lunchboxes, © UFS/King Seeley Thermos/courtesy of FMC; Page 14: Halloween animation cel, gift of Dan Northern/BMP Inc./Lee Mendelson Productions; Pumpkin animation cel, © UFS/BMP/LMP; TV snow globe, courtesy of CA; Jack-o'-lantern sketch, gift of JFS; Page 15: Pumpkin Carols booklet, © UFS/Ambassador Cards/gift of JFS; Pumpkin photo, © The MIT Museum of the Massachusetts Institute of Technology/gift of Brian M. Leibowitz; Animation cel, gift of JFS/BMP Inc./Lee Mendelson Productions; Snoopy sketch, gift of JFS; Page 16: Lucy and Linus campaign images, © UFS/Hallmark Properties, Inc.; Lucy and Linus nodders, © UFS/Determined Productions/courtesy of FMC; Page 17: Lucy and Linus sketch, gift of Jeffery J. Pyros & Robert Casterline; Linus blanket, courtesy of Urban Outfitters; Conversation school book cover, courtesy of Nat Gertler; Lucille letter, © Lucille Ball/gift of JFS; Page 18: Falcon scrapbook, © UFS/Ford Motor Corp/gift of JFS; MetLife images, © UFS/MetLife; Linus, and Lucy Butternut images, © UFS/Butternut Bread/gift of JFS; Snoopy Butternut ad, © UFS/Interstate Brands/courtesy of FMC; Mustang brochure, © UFS/Ford Motor Corp.; Dolly Madison ad, gift of JFS; Page 19: Dolly Madison ad, gift of David Anderson; Page 20: Dynamite cover, © UFS/Scholastic Magazines; Japanese book, courtesy of Nat Gertler; Hike pennant, © UFS/Determined Productions/courtesy of FMC; Page 21: Newsprint sketch, gift of Susan Repke-Rice; Football sketch, gift of JFS; Ceramic Snoopy, © UFS/Determined Productions/courtesy of Donna Nichols Collection; Code book, © UFS/Holt, Rinehart and Winston/gift of JFS; Beagle Power, courtesy of Caren Pilgrim; Page 22: TV Watercolor, © UFS/TV Guide/gift of Jeffrey J. Pyros & Robert

Casterline; Melendez photo, AP Photo/Nick UT; Race frames, gift of JFS/BMP, Inc./ Lee Mendelson Productions; Page 23: Snoopy, Cemetery, and Thanksgiving cels, © UFS/BMP/Lee Mendelson Productions; Storyboard, courtesy of David Guaraldi Collection/BMP, Inc.; Page 24: Charlie and Sally sketch, gift of JFS; Woodstock ornament, © UFS/Determined Productions; Page 25: Joy card, gift of Roy Casstevens; Charlie with cards, gift of JFS; Snow globe, © UFS/Hallmark Cards/gift of Sandy Stec; Album cover, © UFS/Vince Guaraldi/Fantasy Records; Page 26: Daily Dozen cover, © UFS/Hallmark Properties, Inc./gift of JFS; Datebook, © UFS/ Determined Productions, Inc.; Women's Sports cookbook, © Leisure Press, courtesy of Nat Gertler; Bento box, Kaerenmama's Character Bento, published by TAKARAJIMASHA, Inc.; Page 27: Cookbook, courtesy of Nat Gertler; Physics book, © UFS/John Wiley and Sons, Inc./gift of Nancy Nicolelis, David Halliday, and Robert Resnick; Snoopy book and panel, © UFS/Determined Productions, Inc./gift of JFS; Snoopy sushi, courtesy of JFS; Page 28: Doll, © Lego/courtesy of FMC; Bush panel, © Walt Handelsman/courtesy of Tribute Art Collection/gift of Walt Handelsman; Charlie and Pigpen sketch, gift of JFS; Pigpen Patch, courtesy of Caren Pilgrim; Page 29: Recycle panel, © UFS/USA Weekend Magazine/gift of JFS; Page 30: Cel, gift of United Media/BMP, Inc./Lee Mendelson Productions; School Now cover, © UFS/Holt, Rinehart and Winston, Inc.; ABC cover, gift of JFS; Counts cover, gift of JFS; Stamp set, courtesy of Caren Pilgrim; Page 31: Educators panel, gift of JFS; Chinese Dictionary and page, © UFS/RM Enterprises; Valuator cover, © UFS/California Teachers Association/courtesy of Mildred Bettinger; Economic award, gift of JFS/The Advertising Council; Waste basket, © Chein Co./gift of Kansas Museum of History; Page 32: Harp, © UFS/Trophy Music Co./courtesy of FMC/Trophy Music Co.; Electric cover, © UFS/Children's Television Workshop; Page 33: Red Baron cover, © The Royal Guardsmen/Laurie Records/gift of Betty Burns; President cover, © UFS/Vince Guaraldi/Columbia Records/gift of JFS/The Royal Guardsmen/Charles M. Schulz; McKuen cover, © UFS/Rod McKuen/Stanyan Record Co./gift of JFS/Rod McKuen/Charles M. Schulz; Flower cover, courtesy of Nat Gertler; Page 34: Playbill, gift of James Chambers; Souvenir booklet, gift of Jeffery J. Pyros and Robert A. Casterline; Nightclub photo, courtesy of Ken McLaughlin; Cast publicity photo, gift of JFS/John Starr; Page 35: Snoopy poster, courtesy of The Quinn (Larry) Papers; Page 36: Astronaut photo, courtesy NASA; Page 37: Cel, gift of United Media/BMP, Inc.; Project and Apollo decals, courtesy of Charles M. Schulz/ NASA/Vitachrome, Inc.; Flying doll photo, gift of The Boeing Company/NASA; Patch, gift of JFS/Charles M. Schulz/NASA; Page 38: Book sketch and strip, gift of JFS; Page 39: Ornament, © UFS/Determined Productions/gift of Jacquie Bailey; Cel, © UFS/BMP/LMP; Cheering strip, gift of JFS; Page 40: Woodstock sketch, gift of JFS; Baseball doll, © UFS/Determined Productions; Page 41: Tennis Love book, © UFS/Macmillan Publishing Co./courtesy of Billie Jean King/Charles M. Schulz; Baseball cards, © UFS/Interstate Brands/courtesy of FMC/Interstate Brands; San Francisco magazine, © UFS/San Francisco Magazine/courtesy of Vince Guaraldi

Collection/gift of David Guaraldi; Sebastopol albums, gift of Neil Yeager; Charlie hockey figurine, courtesy of photographer D.J. Ashton; Snoopy with sports gear, gift of JFS; Page 42: Animation cel, © UFS/BMP/LMP; Page 43: Marcy sketch, gift of JFS; Patty, Shermy, and Violet magnets, © UFS/Simple Simon/courtesy of FMC; Animation cel, © UFS/BMP/LMP/gift of Jeffery J. Pyros & Robert Casterline/ BMP, Inc./LMP; Butternut sketch, © UFS/Interstate Brands/gift of JFS; Charlotte Braun letter, © CMS, Courtesy Library of Congress Page 44: Nature poster, gift of JFS; Doghouse drawing, gift of JFS; Pollution bookmark, courtesy of Anderson (Clayton) Collection/U.S. Department of the Interior; Carter letter, gift of JFS/Jimmy Carter; Horizon poster, courtesy of Anderson (Clayton) Collection/Gift of Clayton Anderson/U.S. Department of the Interior; Storyboard, © UFS/American Lung Association; Page 45: Woodstock poster, courtesy of Anderson (Clayton) Collection/ Gift of Clayton Anderson/U.S. Department of the Interior; Tree bookmark, courtesy of New York State Arbor Day Committee; Eye patch booklet, courtesy of Nat Gertler Page 46: Piano Guild cover, © UFS/National Guild of Piano Teachers; Page 47: Music box, © UFS/Anri Schmid; Napkin, © UFS/Monogram/gift of Terry & Keith Wicks; Page 48: PVC Franklin, gift of CA; Glickman letter, © and gift of Ms. Harriet R. Glickman; All About cover, © UFS/Fawcett Publications/gift of Donna Nichols/ Jeffrey H. Loria; Good Things cover, © UFS/Tropper Books/courtesy of Abraham J. Twerski (M.D.); Page 49: Tree panel, gift of JFS; Page 50: Red-haired girl sketch, gift of JFS; Lucy banner, © UFS/Determined Productions/courtesy of FMC; Page 51: Valentine letter, gift to CMSM; Sally & Linus figurines, © UFS/Determined Productions, courtesy of Caren Pilgrim; Press release images, courtesy of Caren Pilgrim Page 52: Olaf doll, © UFS/Determined Productions/gift of CA; Spike sketches, gift of JFS; Needles letter, gift of JFS/City of Needles, California; Andy doll, © UFS/Determined Productions/gift of CA; Torn strip, gift of JFS; Page 53: Spike doll, © Tomy/courtesy of CMSM Product Collection/Gift of CA; Spike watercolor, CMSM Art Collection, Page 54: Everhart poster, © UFS/Tom Everhart/ Fusosha; Museum poster, courtesy of Norman Rockwell Museum; Parade sculpture, courtesy of Laughing Squid; Louvre poster, courtesy of Ruby Persson; Page 55: Snoopy art, gift of JFS; Page 56: Linus and Lucy storyboard, gift of JFS/BMP, Inc.; Rerun sketches, gift of JFS; Sally baby doll, © UFS/Hungerford Plastics Corp./gift of Allison Perrin; Sally School cover, © UFS/Sparkler Books/gift of JFS; Page 57: Sally doll, courtesy CA; Page 58: Schulz at desk, courtesy of Brian Lanker; Medal, gift of JFS/U.S. Congress; Grief panel, © Steve Kelly/San Diego Union Tribune; Page 59: Schulz with doll, gift of JFS; Signatures, gift of JFS; Christmas poster, gift of JFS and Redwood Empire Ice Arena; Farewell strip, © Milwaukee Journal Sentinel; Medal, gift of JFS/U.S. Congress; Page 60: All, courtesy of CMSM; Page 61: Museum visitor book cover, photography by D.J. Ashton; Page 62: Children at museum, © Annee Booker Knight; Museum images, courtesy of CMSM; Page 63: Hard hat, photography by D.J. Ashton. Page 64: © UFS/Random House School Division.